I SHALL BECOME OF YOUR DREAMS?

Parable of the Sponge Ball:
The harder you get knocked down,
the higher you bounce back.

Gladston Cuffie

What Shall Become of Your Dreams
Trilogy Christian Publishers A Wholly Owned Subsidiary of Trinity Broadcasting Network
2442 Michelle Drive Tustin, CA 92780
Copyright © 2022 by Gladston Cuffie

Scripture quotations marked NLT are taken from the Holy Bible, New Living Translation, copyright © 1996, 2004, 2015 by Tyndale House Foundation. Used by permission of Tyndale House Publishers, Inc., Carol Stream, Illinois 60188. All rights reserved.
Scripture quotations marked TLB are taken from The Living Bible copyright © 1971. Used by permission of Tyndale House Publishers, a Division of Tyndale House Ministries, Carol Stream, Illinois 60188. All rights reserved.
Scripture quotations marked KJV are taken from the King James Version of the Bible. Public domain.

No part of this book may be reproduced, stored in a retrieval system, or transmitted by any means without written permission from the author. All rights reserved. Printed in the USA.
Rights Department, 2442 Michelle Drive, Tustin, CA 92780.
Trilogy Christian Publishing/TBN and colophon are trademarks of Trinity Broadcasting Network.
For information about special discounts for bulk purchases, please contact Trilogy Christian Publishing.
Trilogy Disclaimer: The views and content expressed in this book are those of the author and may not necessarily reflect the views and doctrine of Trilogy Christian Publishing or the Trinity Broadcasting Network.

Manufactured in the United States of America
10 9 8 7 6 5 4 3 2 1
Library of Congress Cataloging-in-Publication Data is available.
ISBN: 978-1-63769-830-3
E-ISBN: 978-1-63769-831-0

Dedication

Dedicated to the memory of my wife, Shelly-Ann Cuffie.

If nobody is perfect, then Shelly-Ann got the closest to perfection that is possible.

Contents

Introduction 7

Chapter 1: A Dream Never Dies 9

Chapter 2: The Fuel of Dreams 21

Chapter 3: Relationship Dreams 33

Chapter 4: Life After Mistakes 45

Chapter 5: The Flipside of Love 53

Chapter 6: A Rocky Road 69

Chapter 7: Starting Over 81

Chapter 8: Just Release It 93

Chapter 9: Battered and Bruised but Still a Winner 109

Chapter 10: Encourage Yourself 123

Chapter 11: I Feel Invisible 139

Chapter 12: Majoring in Minors 153

Chapter 13: Please Don't Judge Me 169

Chapter 14: Against All Odds 185

Chapter 15: Mistaken Identity 197

Introduction

One of the reasons Jesus was such an effective communicator was because He used a lot of parables. In simple terms, a parable is a story that uses a well-known principle to explain or teach a deep moral or spiritual lesson. In this book, I use the Parable of the Sponge Ball.

When a ball is knocked down, it bounces back. The harder it is knocked down, the higher it bounces back. I use this principle to represent our lives and our dreams. We will all get knocked down at some point. And when we do, we will never achieve our dreams if we do not bounce back.

When a ball is being knocked down, potential energy is converted to kinetic energy, which is the energy an object has when it is moving. The faster an object moves (or the harder it is knocked down), the higher its kinetic energy, and that energy helps it bounce back. Therefore, if your life is like a sponge ball, being knocked down gives you the kinetic energy you need to bounce back higher.

So see yourself as a sponge ball. You have dreams. Sometimes you will get knocked down and your dreams will be in danger of dying. But because you are like a sponge ball, you will bounce back; and the harder you get knocked down, the higher

What Shall We Become of Your Dreams

you bounce back. It becomes impossible to keep you down. You will get knocked down but never get knocked out.

The title of the book is inspired by Genesis Chapter 37.

Joseph's brothers said,
"Look, the dreamer is coming, let us kill him.
And we shall see what will become of his dreams."[1]

Throughout the book, I tell a lot of true stories. In every case, the names are either disguised or omitted to protect the privacy of the individuals, most of whom, or their relatives, are still alive.

Enjoy!

---

1 *Genesis 37:18-20 NLT*

Chapter 1

A DREAM NEVER DIES

"You are living your best life. You feel like dancing. You break out in singing songs of praise whenever you can. You can identify with the saying, 'I made it through the rain.'"

A Dream Never Dies

I was only twenty-four years old. I had just completed building my dream house. It was literally the achievement of a dream because since I was a pre-teen child, I used to draw a house design in the sand of the yard at our childhood home. I would point to a nearby vacant parcel of land, and looking at the finger-drawing in the sand, I would say to my siblings, "I will build this house on that land." Now as a young adult, I built the house in the same design that I used to draw in the sand on the same parcel of land to which I used to point as a child.

One afternoon an elderly man – he was much older than I was – dropped in to say hello to me and to see my just-completed house. I estimated that he was over fifty years old because he was the father of a friend with whom I had gone to school, plus he was grey-haired and balding.

He walked all around, both inside and outside the house and congratulated me on my achievement. During the conversation, he made a particular statement that I have never forgotten. He did not realize it, but it was a loaded statement. The impact of his comment only hit after he had left and I was reflecting on his visit and our conversation. He said, "When I build my own house, I want to build something just like this."

Most likely you are wondering what is the big deal with that statement. This is the big deal. Here I was at twenty-four years of age talking to a man who was more than twice my age, who

What Shall We Become of Your Dreams

could have been my father, and he was saying "when" he builds his house. He didn't say "if I could build a house"; he said when. Clearly, he had a dream. And that dream was still burning in his heart.

I was a banker at the time, and I was working in the mortgage company. My job was working with people who were applying for mortgages to build or buy their homes. I knew a little of how the process worked. So when I reflected on the gentleman's statement, I thought, "At his age, how is he going to get a mortgage? Surely, if he had the funds to finance it himself, he would have done it already." It appeared to me as if it was difficult or unlikely that his dream could come to pass.

But to him, it was still a dream. And then it hit me: a dream never dies. As long as one is alive and conscious, a dream is in the heart.

> *Dream*
> *Noun*
>
> 1. *A mental picture of what one wants to become or achieve. A cherished aspiration; a goal or objective.*
>
> 2. *Thoughts, images or experiences that seem to occur in a person's mind during sleep.*

It is definition number one that this gentleman was experiencing. And it could be the most powerful driving force in a person's

A Dream Never Dies

life. To dream is to live. If one doesn't have a dream, one is just existing – just drifting through life.

But the person with a dream wakes up every day driven to achieve something – to take an action, make a decision, or do something to get closer to the dream. The dream is at the forefront of one's mind, pushing one to make sacrifices and expend extraordinary energy along with constant evaluation, self-reflection, and measurement to keep track of progress.

And there is where one of life's biggest challenges occurs. Because your dream consumes you, and your whole life is built around attempts to achieve your dream, very intense emotional energy is invested in the pursuit of it. And if the dream appears to be collapsing or slipping away, it could be one of life's most disappointing and distressing seasons. It can take a major emotional toll on one's life. It can drive one to cynicism, frustration, or depression.

A broken dream can cause some people to become bitter and resentful; they look at the success of others and feel pain while they silently whisper to themselves, "So what's wrong with me? Why can't I do that?" Sometimes they cast blame on others who blocked their dream and feel hate and anger towards them. Some give up on a meaningful life and settle for just going through the motions of life every day. They cannot muster the emotional strength or self-confidence to fight again. They are knocked

What Shall We Become of Your Dreams

down and they feel beaten and broken.

At some point, we will all be confronted by the question, "What shall become of your dreams?" It is in these moments we must reflect on the parable of the sponge ball. Life may have knocked you down. Mischievous people may have undermined you. But you must say, "I may have made mistakes that set me back. Circumstances, bad judgment, or misfortune may have knocked me down. But I am a sponge ball: when I get knocked down, I bounce back. And when I get knocked down harder, I bounce back higher.

"I am going to go back to my dream. I will achieve it. I am the bounce-back kid."

You see, many people have unrealistic expectations. They make the mistake of thinking that achieving a dream is smooth sailing. It hardly ever is. But God, working with your faith, your genuine efforts, your persistence, and your inner strength, will take you to your destination. Most times, what looks like a setback and what is very disappointing and painful, eventually turns out to be a steppingstone.

Your dream is likely to attract envy. Your dream is likely to attract hate. Your dream is likely to attract saboteurs. And all of these are likely to become more intense when your dream starts to visibly manifest.

A Dream Never Dies

The Lifecycle of a Dream

There is something I call the lifecycle of a dream.

Stage 1:
Birth

The stage when the dream enters your heart. You start to see visions of your desired state in your mind.

And you are quietly saying, "That's it. That's what I want to do. That's where I want to go. I can do that. That will be my best life."

You jump off your bed with a pep in your step. You feel ready for the world. There's a fire in your bones.

Stage 2:
Journey

You start to position yourself. You talk to others. You read. You do research. You acquire skills. You get training. You pray. You fast.

You keep your eyes and ears open for opportunities. And you jump at opportunities when you see them.

And you are on your way.

Stage 3:
Struggle

This is the sponge-ball phase. You keep getting knocked down. But you have to keep bouncing back.

You make mistakes. You encounter haters. You meet unanticipated hurdles. You run into negative people. You get discouraged. You endure discrimination.

What Shall We Become of Your Dreams

But you also meet some really helpful people; people who appear to have been sent by God, and often they are. People who are so genuine and selfless, you don't understand why they are so kind.

And in your silent moments, you shed a tear or two. And it's bitter-sweet: the struggles make you cry, and the gratitude for people who help you also makes you cry. But it's a different emotion with the tears of gratitude; it is one of thankfulness.

And at the end of the day, you say, "Lord, I just want to thank You."

Stage 4: *Achievement* You learned from your struggles. All of the drama of Stage 3 went into creating a you that ultimately moved you to the place of your dream.

You won! And you look at yourself with self-satisfaction and pride. You are living your best life.

You feel like dancing. You break out in singing songs of praise whenever you can. You can identify with the saying, "I made it through the rain" or "There was another in the fire."

And you know in your heart that God is good. And you give praise.

16

Let me illustrate this with an example with which most people are familiar, and told in my own words: David versus Goliath.[2]

Stage 1: Birth

David was coming into town to bring food for his brothers. He was just a little boy who was only trusted with the simple task of looking after sheep.

He observed that the town was deserted. People were scared of Goliath. They were dispirited and out of options for defeating Goliath. His people were on the brink of a major defeat, possibly obliteration by Goliath.

And at that moment, his dream was born: "I can do this. I can fight this battle and win. I can beat Goliath."

Stage 2: Journey

He started to talk to people and ask questions. "Why is this un-circumcised Philistine allowed to threaten us? Tell me again, what is the King's offer? I heard there is a reward for defeating Goliath. Is that true?"

He examined his skills and abilities. He was confident because he had fought and won against a lion and a bear. He had experienced how God can give someone an advantage is a situation that seems impossible.

---

2 1 Samuel 17

Stage 3: Struggle

David had to endure the inevitable struggle that comes with pursuing a dream. His older brother tried to humiliate him: "Why are you here? You are just excessively curious about what's not your business. How could you leave the few sheep you were watching?" He made sure to say "few sheep" to rub in the insinuation that David was only capable of minor responsibilities and had no place in a time of major crisis.

And then there was King Saul: "David, you can't do this. You are not trained. You are just a little boy. You are no match for Goliath. He was fighting since he was your age, and he is now a grown man."

David had to fight off humiliation from his brother and lack of confidence from the King. But he had a dream. He was probably wondering, "With all this negativity, what shall become of my dream?"

Stage 4: Achievement

David was like the sponge ball. He had to bounce back from humiliation. He had to bounce back from the rebuke from his brother. He had to bounce back from the king's lack of confidence in him. Nobody thought David could do it.

A Dream Never Dies

Except him.

But he won! And he became a hero for all time.

Be like David. Believe in yourself.

And when you get knocked down, bounce back.

The harder you get knocked down just means that you are bouncing back higher.

Chapter 2

THE FUEL OF DREAMS

"Failure is easy. It is easier to fail an exam than to pass one. It is easier to break something than to build it. One can just be idle, drop out of school, pay no attention to excellence on the job, shun self-development, and one would fail."

The Fuel of Dreams

In Chapter 1, I mentioned that I was able to

complete my dream house before I was twenty-five years old. That is not typical in my environment; it is indeed a notable achievement, and I praise God for His favor.

Many times, testimonies and stories about the fulfillment of dreams are like that. We get the high points and it appears to be very easy. But the road to fulfilling great dreams has a lot of bumps, twists, and turns. This what I call Stage Three, the Struggle Stage.

My homeownership dream started with acquiring the parcel of land that I had looked at since I was a child. That was a long and difficult process. There were numerous visits to different offices, legal issues, disappointments, and blocked paths. Government ministries had to get involved. I wrote to several people, some of whom didn't bother to reply or acknowledge my letters.

Ultimately, a government ministry was required to send a note to the national cabinet to get a decision to make the parcel of land available for me to purchase. I was an unknown young man, from a poor family, in what was a rural community at the time, who had to have this matter decided by the cabinet – the highest governmental level! What are the odds?

This took a couple of years. And many letters. And many meetings. And many hours in waiting rooms. And many hours of

What Shall We Become of Your Dreams

driving to different offices. And many disappointments. But eventually, I was able to purchase the land.

After that, I applied and was able to secure a mortgage to build the house. But...

When it was time to build, I engaged a contractor who turned out to be less than honest, and he was doing poor quality work. At one time, a retaining wall that was five feet high and one hundred and twenty-five feet long, collapsed and broke into pieces with the first shower of rain that came after it was completed. I had to fire the contractor. That led to a dispute and threats of legal action. It took months to resolve, and the project stalled for some time.

Later, an employee with the roofing contractor fell about thirty feet off the roof onto the ground below. He survived, but the roofer quit the job. I had to complete the roofing work myself with only the knowledge that I gained by just watching him work during the time he was on the job.

And in trying to complete the roof, perhaps because of inexperience, I slipped and was going down about forty feet below where there were debris of boulders, boards with nails in them, and pieces of steel. I didn't know if I would have survived that fall. But by God's grace and divine protection, I stretched out my hand, and in a split second, I was able to grab a part of the

The Fuel of Dreams

roof that was protruding and pull myself up.

So my dream to build my house was achieved. But I had to overcome many obstacles and bounce back from a lot of disappointments. In the story of my house, one can identify the four stages of a dream: Birth, Journey, Struggle, and Achievement.

So what shall become of *your* dream?

Failure is Easy

Dreams have certain characteristics. They are usually big and difficult to envision if one looks at the limitations of one's present circumstances. David was about five feet tall; Goliath was about nine feet tall. David had no experience as a fighter; Goliath was a life-long warrior.

And this is true even in managing a secular career or a business, whether it is a small business or a large corporation. When a company develops vision and mission statements, they invest a lot of resources to ensure that the employees understand their true meaning. The vision statement is an aspiration for the future state of the company. It is the company's dream. In almost every case it is not a routine objective that could be achieved by simply going through normal paces. It requires a quantum leap, a transformational journey to reach the desired state. And for it to work, every employee must know the vision and be committed

What Shall We Become of Your Dreams

to it. All other plans, strategies, and tactics of the company must be aligned to the vision and mission. If they are just beautifully framed "pieces of paper" on the wall, they are unlikely to be achieved.

In the same way, your personal goal – your dream – must be aligned with your life. You must be consciously taking specific steps towards it.

But even so, dreams are clearest to the dreamer. Often, others will be unable to accept that it can be achieved. They cannot see what you see because what you see is in your mind and in your heart. That is the reason the person with a dream almost always encounters cynicism from others. David's brother rebuked him. Saul told him he did not stand a chance.

Dreams don't come true easily. The world's best athletes don't just casually make it to the top of the rostrum. They spend hours of each day in the gym, in training. They watch their diets. They watch everything that they eat or drink. They watch how much sleep they get. They set goals. They measure themselves against the best in the world.

It's called focus. It's called discipline.

Do you realize that it is easier to be a failure than it is to be a success? Failure is easy. It is easier to fail an exam than to pass one. It is easier to lose a job than to find one. It is easier to break

The Fuel of Dreams

something than to build it. One doesn't have to expend any effort or make any sacrifices to fail. One can just be idle, drop out of school, pay no attention to excellence on the job, refuse training, shun self-development, and one would fail.

Laziness is not the fuel of dreams. Sloppiness does not fuel dreams. Mediocrity does not fuel dreams. They fuel failure. Many people fail because it is very easy to fail; just do nothing, or do what you do poorly.

Success, on the other hand, takes strength, discipline, and courage. To achieve the dream of certification, you have to spend a lot of time "hitting the books." To be prepared for the examinations, you have to forgo some other things that you would otherwise be doing.

To develop a successful career, you have to be committed to excellence and continuous self-improvement; you have to understand corporate expectations, learn good people skills, how to be a team-player, and just know how to get along. You have to work on your communication skills and style; know how to persuade, how to make a convincing argument. You have to learn temperament control and respect for others.

To develop a stable spiritual life, you need to spend time in the Word of God, spend time in regular fellowship, spend time in prayer and fasting, and have respect for divine offices in the church. You need to cleanse your heart from human weaknesses like hate, unforgiveness, grudges, and bitterness. One of the most powerful but little-known prescriptions given by David is found in 2 Samuel 22, "The Lord rewarded my according to my righteousness: according to the cleanness of my hands in his eyesight."[3] There is a correlation between the condition of the heart and the blessings of God that lead to success.

Achieving your dreams; achieving success, does not come without a vision, a clear focus and the willingness to put in the required effort and make sacrifices. I referred earlier to the favor of God upon my academic achievements and my career. Just to encourage a dreamer who is reading this, I testify of this: the blessings did not come arbitrarily; God doesn't play favorites.

It's Not Magic

During my first five years of secondary school, I was never absent once. I never cut classes either. Once, I was knocked down by a car on the way to school but I went to the hospital, got my hands bandaged up, and went to school afterward. Thanks be to God, there was no serious damage. Another time, I went to the hospital for a minor surgery on one eye. I got the surgery, got my eye-patch bandage, and went to school after I left the hospital – with one eye covered-up. I looked like a pirate, but I was in school. On the job, I averaged about one sick day a year for ten years (probably for most of my career too, but I can't recall).

3 *2 Samuel 22:25 KJV*

The Fuel of Dreams

At one time, I attended a church that had services four times a week, and another special service once monthly, but I never missed any of the services in seven years (apart from short periods when I was out of the country). Blessings, favor, and success do not come like magic. You have to invest in them.

One of God's criterion for success is that you must be doing something. He cannot bless nothing. He cannot multiply nothing. Even if He does, nothing multiplied by nothing gives nothing. The proof is in Deuteronomy 28, where He promises to bless the *work* of your hands. You have to work. And it is also in Psalm 1, where David describes how a successful person gets blessed by saying, "whatsoever they *do* shall prosper."[4] You have to be doing something.

Many of us are misled into wanting big successes or breakthroughs when pursuing our dreams without any tangible, provable, or measurable input into it. It doesn't work that way. One cannot just wish for great things. One cannot hope to simply "get lucky." One cannot just simply say, "I'm trusting God" or "I'm believing" or indeed "I'm praying about it." Praying, believing, and hoping are all part of the believer's toolkit. But they must all be backed up by doing. Whatsoever you *do* shall prosper.

Let us consult James on this matter:

---

4 Psalm 1:3 KJV

What Shall We Become of Your Dreams

What good is it dear brothers and sisters, if you say you have faith but you don't show it by your actions. Faith by itself isn't good enough. Unless it produces good deeds, it is dead and useless. You know, someone may argue some people have faith but do not have good deeds. But I say how can you show me your faith if you don't have good deeds. I will show you my faith by my good deeds.

You say you have faith for you believe there is one God. Good for you! Even the demons believe this and they tremble in terror. How foolish! Can't you see that faith without good deeds is useless? Remember that Abraham was shown to be right with God by his actions. You see, his faith and his actions worked together. His actions made his faith complete.[5]

Then there is confidence. Confidence is the fuel of dreams. But you need to be clear about the basis of your confidence. When your confidence is in God, you have your priorities right. David was clear. He confidently proclaimed that whereas Goliath's confidence was in his own skills, abilities, and tools of war, he (David) depended on the Lord his God.

In my case, completing my house at twenty-four years is a wonderful story.

---

5 James 2:14-21 NLT

The Fuel of Dreams

But I have served God since the age of eighteen.

I was using all my talents and resources to contribute to the kingdom of God from that age.

I had a divine partner.

The favor of God underwrites a dream.

Chapter 3

RELATIONSHIP DREAMS

"When relationship dreams fail, there is a constant confrontation between the human in us and the pain in us. The pain wants us to remain fearful and distrustful. But the human wants us to move on, to believe that 'happily ever after' is still achievable."

Relationship Dreams

What is the most beautiful thing in the world?

Love is the most beautiful thing in the world. Love is the basis of every other beautiful thing that there is: marriage, children, friendship, siblings, patriotism, etc. Love is manifested in relationships. Indeed, at the heart of God's plan for man and the basis of God's relationship with His people is the verse that starts, "For God so loved..."[6]

In the biblical story of creation, after every step of His work, God reflected on what He did and then He said, "Good job!" Over and over, after each step of creation, God was pleased with His work, declaring, "Good job!" But there was one point at which He paused, reflected, and said, "This is not good." That was after He created a man as the only human. God concluded that creating a man alone was a bad idea. So He created a woman for the man.

God created the concept of human relationships.

Let us understand the context in which God concluded that it was not good for a (hu)man to live alone. The earth was spanking new and unspoiled; everything was in pristine condition; the environment was perfect. The earth was very fertile and productive. The streams of water were pure. The trees were lush green. There was no pollution, no global warming, no vehicle emissions. The man had the company of God Himself; he was able

---

6 John 3:16 KJV

What Shall We Become of Your Dreams

to hang out with God. The devil didn't yet make an appearance! There was no sin. Yet, despite this perfect environment, God thought that the missing link was a relationship.

Relationships make a perfect life "more perfect."

The love of one person for another is one of the most powerful and binding experiences of the human existence. Loneliness is not good simply because it speaks to the absence of other people in someone's life. The cure for loneliness is the availability of another person, or other people, to love or to share some aspects of our lives. I would argue that the most valuable thing that one person can give to another is love. It's not the things we do, or the things we give, because it is love that motivates the giving or the doing.

The quality of our relationships is the quality of our lives.

An Imaginary Journey

Harvard University researchers conducted the Grant Study, an eighty-year study of a group of men. The objective of the study was to follow human development over their lifetime with the hope of identifying specific attributes that would enable the researchers to gain an understanding of what contributes to having a fulfilling life.

After more than eighty years and significant financial invest-

Relationship Dreams

ments, the researchers concluded that the key requirement for a human being to have a fulfilling life was love – strong, loving relationships. It was not material possessions, prestige, or riches that made life meaningful.

Good relationships are considered as important as diet and exercise. And the negative effects of loneliness are comparable to smoking and alcoholism.

For the academically inclined, it may now be a little clearer why God said it is not good for a human to be alone (lonely).

Love is a consequence of human relationships. Clearly, a major objective for all of us should be to live a life of love. Unfortunately, many of us get misled into having our priorities mixed-up, chasing a lot of short-term, temporary things, and even if we do achieve them, they do not contribute to the quality of our lives if we look deep inside our hearts without any filters or pretensions. It is not that things like money and prestige are not important; it is that they do not have the same depth of meaning if they are not accompanied by love.

Most people would appreciate increasing their wealth, or increasing the amount of assets that they own to help them live comfortably. There are many firms and careers built on the premise of wealth creation, asset management, and investment management. The objective of all of these is ultimately to im-

What Shall We Become of Your Dreams

prove the financial situation of individuals or corporations.

So imagine you own your home debt-free. Then imagine you own the whole street that you live on, and then you own your town, then you own your country, and then everything in the whole world. What if you own all the riches, all the property, everything that you could imagine: the beautiful waterfalls, the airplanes, the skyscrapers, the diamonds, the restaurants, everything? You own it all.

And then imagine that there is nobody else in the world but you.

How happy would you be? My guess is that if a person owns the whole world but is in it all alone, that person will not want to live and will rapidly suffer some type of breakdown and die. My point is that relationships make us happy, not what we possess. Therefore, the pursuit of love before we pursue things is wise. Things without people we love with which to share them are meaningless. Love should be the primary objective of every human being.

Now if I ask you to describe the happiest moments of your life and the worst moments of your life, what would those be? Both your best and worst moments are likely to involve some type of relationship.

People have relationship dreams too. Because relationships are at the core of our happiness.

Relationship Dreams

Since relationships are a fundamental part of our lives, when they fail there is much pain and tears. In conversing with people over the years, some of the saddest stories I have heard came from broken or dysfunctional relationships. These include not just romantic or intimate relationships but any type of relationship where one person trusts another or expected a high standard of moral, ethical, or honest conduct from another person. It is also among siblings and relatives, seniors or colleagues on the job, or with an authority figure such as a teacher, a religious leader, a public figure like a judge or someone in public office.

When these relationships fail, you experience things like betrayal, abuse, discrimination, deceit, and any manner of a breach of trust or emotional manipulation. Bouncing back from this type of pain is one of life's most daunting challenges.

The Language of Pain

This is a conversation that I had with a woman who said she was completely faithful and very happy in her marriage, only to find out that she was being deceived and manipulated by a dishonest husband. She eventually got divorced. This is a true story, reproduced verbatim from my WhatsApp chat. Here is her emotional outlook on life:

Once upon a time, I was contented. I was very focused on my family. I now choose to live alone because I had bad experi-

ences. I don't want to live alone but I'm scared. I'm scared of feeling pressure; pressure is created out of expectations. People have different expectations of how a life partner should be. I don't know if I can meet those expectations.

Relationships are different. People tend to compare previous relationships and previous families. I have had so much disappointment from both relationships and family, I just don't want to be hurt. I choose not to bring anyone into my life. I am not prepared for anyone to leave me homeless. People around me seem to have very weak minds.

I prefer not to let an irresponsible person into my life. I live alone and I feel safe. People do not understand what commitment is. I committed my emotions, my time, my heart, my love, and look where I am now, alone! Someone in an intimate relationship could cost you your peace of mind, especially if that person does not appreciate your trust.

It's different when you're a woman. You have to know who you befriend because men see things as opportunities. I can only imagine the plight of women who are not strong and financially independent. Men would make a woman feel like trash because she is in need. That's why I work so many long hours.

That's a lot to take in. Read it again. But that was the pain talking

Relationship Dreams

because later in that same conversation, she said: "I am tired of living alone. It's so hard to live alone. I need a life. I'm ready. I am prepared to meet someone; someone who I can love, someone who could love me, someone who can make me happy. I'm ready for a new start to my life." These statements reflected the real human being; the real woman talking. A woman, like all other women, who needs the joy of a loving relationship.

When relationship dreams fail, there is a constant confrontation between the human in us and the pain in us. The pain wants us to remain fearful and distrustful. And alone. But the human in us wants us to move on, to believe that the second time would not be like the first, like "happily ever after" is still achievable. We know we have as much love to give as we want to receive, but we have to battle with the pain. And the fear. And the insecurity.

The woman quoted earlier needed to reclaim her lost dream. It was a perfect case of someone asking, "What shall become of my dreams?" Her dream of a loving, fulfilling, romantic life appeared to be lost. She needed to bounce back. So this was part of my response to help her bounce back higher:

First, I believe that people are not designed to live alone for a long time. Second, not all men are selfish and manipulative. Good men still exist.

You talk a lot about enjoying being alone. Sometimes people can become so accustomed to a particular way of relating to the world that it becomes part of their personality, and then they have difficulty adjusting. So you need to consider whether you can adjust to being focused on a committed relationship without missing what you describe as the freedom of being alone.

If you don't clarify those feelings, you can commit to someone and then feel like you're missing "the freedom of being alone," which can lead to you being unhappy and unstable in the relationship.

Being in a committed relationship is a big life change. Whereas there are so many benefits in a happy relationship, it is a big change that you have to think about carefully.

You have a lot going for you. You have kept yourself stable despite your difficulties. You survived major adversities. You are a good communicator. You have a sense of humor.

Now it is time to clear your mind and focus on your future. Don't let the experiences of the past be baggage that you drag but let them be lessons your learned. And move forward to love again. That is my advice.

Those experiences that you've had are lessons that you can use to make the next time amazing. You shouldn't let them make you suspicious of every future relationship. Our past experiences influence how we see future relationships but

Relationship Dreams

they should be teachers, not slave masters.

We all have to make sure that we don't punish future people for the sins of past people. If that happens, we carry past pain into future relationships and relive the past all over again.

You have to dig deep to examine what your inner self really wants. I'm just poking you to look at your inner self so that you could give attention to what your inner self really wants. One can lose the future by being chained to the past.

The only way you can again find love, romance, and all those nice things is if you "take a chance" and open your heart to love. You cannot love with a closed heart. However, it's not literally a chance because you get to know someone, you get to evaluate and assess a relationship before you commit to it.

Use the accumulated wisdom gained from the past, even the painful past, to inform your judgment about a future relationship. But you have to be clear in your heart about what you want and make it open to give and receive love.

Be cautious. Be wise.
But don't be a prisoner of the past.
There's a lovely world of love waiting to be found.
But there's not a lot of time.

Chapter 4

LIFE AFTER MISTAKES

"You may feel embarrassed. You may have made a fool of yourself. You ask yourself a million times, 'How could I have been so stupid?' You know that letting-down others is disappointing. But disappointing yourself is on another level."

Life After Mistakes

Jane was a young professional working with a strong company. She was a colleague whose workstation was just a few feet away from mine. She was an attractive woman who had good potential to excel and move up the corporate ladder. From all appearances, she had a normal successful life and a promising career.

Then I started to hear rumors.

As we know, rumors are part of life, and the office is a fertile ground for rumors. At some stage, most adults have been on the receiving end of rumors.

But back to Jane. I was hearing other colleagues whispering about her private life; how her marriage had fallen apart and she was now living with a married man whom she had "stolen." I always had a distaste for rumors. My creed was, and still is, if I have a good rapport with someone and I hear unflattering things, I would let the person know what was being said. I wouldn't create confusion by revealing the source, but by letting someone know, that person could address it if they wished. I would also have the benefit of the other side of the story if the person chooses to clarify.

So I spoke to Jane. Her response was brief and blunt. I was taken aback a bit. Perhaps that is why so many years later, I still clearly remember it. She said, "Another woman stole my husband, so I

What Shall We Become of Your Dreams

don't care if I have to steal somebody's husband!"

The pain of losing a relationship dream can make us do strange things. We lash out. We get bitter. We seek revenge. We hurt others. We justify dysfunctional behaviour. We see right as wrong and wrong as right. We resist advice and counsel. We can become very messed-up when we get badly hurt.

But none of these helps us bounce back. Quite the opposite. All of these put us deeper in a state of despair. We are more likely to cause long-term harm to our reputation and seriously compromise our chances of bouncing back.

One of the most influential persons who ever lived is the person we know as the Apostle Paul. Paul had a very simple but powerful approach to achieving his best life. He simply said, "I forget those things which are behind me and I press forward to fulfill my destiny."[7] Your best days can be ahead of you if you leave some of the drama of the past and focus on the pursuit of a bright new future.

Consider this. What do you do if you accidentally hold on to something that is very hot? Instinctively, the body's built-in defense system kicks in and you instantly drop the hot object and pull away. If you do not let it drop as quickly as possible, you get seriously hurt and if you survive, you get scarred for the rest of your life.

---

7 *Philippians 3:13 (paraphrased)*

Life After Mistakes

It's easier to get back on the path to your dream if you release yourself from the weight of past hurts, and instead map out a plan for your future. Holding on to the "hot objects" of pain, failure, mistakes, betrayal, or disappointments could cost you your life or leave you with permanent scars.

David got entrapped in some of the worst aspects of human weaknesses (2 Samuel): duplicity, deceitfulness, sexual sin, and murder. It could hardly get worse than that. But when the seriousness of his conduct was revealed to him, he quickly "fessed up," dropped the "hot object," and acknowledged his wrongdoing. He then used his failures to give guidance to future generations on how to talk to God when one is truly sorry for one's actions.

Be the person who doesn't let a mistake, regardless of how grave, turn you into a failure. There is life after mistakes.

You may feel embarrassed. You may have made a fool of yourself. You may feel like hiding from friends and relatives. You ask yourself a million times, "How could I have been so stupid? How could I let that happen to me?" You know that letting-down others is disappointing. But letting-down yourself is on another level.

But quitting won't make any of this go away. Quitting won't get you back on the path to your dream. Bouncing back is the best antidote for stupid mistakes. Get up and get moving. Today.

The Rock and the Pebble

The story is told of a man who went to a pastor and said, "Pastor, not even God could help me. I have lived a terrible life. I messed up over and over. I hurt people. I was selfish and destructive. I am well known and I am despised because of my misdeeds. And I am just telling you my good parts!"

The pastor took him for a walk outside next to a pond and asked him to follow some simple instructions: "Take up that little pebble on the ground next to your foot, throw it in the pond and describe what you see and hear."

The man did as he was asked, threw the pebble in the pond, and described, "I hear a faint sound when the pebble hit the water. I see some little ripples in the water, and I see the pebble moving slowly down, and now it is resting at the bottom of the pond."

Then the pastor gave another instruction, "Now take the large rock on the other side, throw it in the pond, and describe what you see and hear."

The man complied. "I hear a loud sound, I see a big splash and huge waves in the water. Eventually, I see the rock settled next to the pebble at the bottom of the pond."

Life After Mistakes

The pastor then said, "Here's the moral of the story. Some people make small mistakes; commit small sins, if you want to use that word. Their mistakes hardly have any impact and are not noticed by many people, if anybody at all. They don't make waves. That is the pebble.

"Other people make huge mistakes, their mistakes are seen and heard by lots of people. They make a lot of waves and disrupt a lot of people's lives. They are featured on the news. That is the rock that was thrown in the pool. But ultimately, both the pebble and the large rock settle at the bottom of the pond; the sea of forgetfulness.

"You are like the rock. It all depends on what you want to do with your big mistakes and your big sins. If you acknowledge them and let God bury them in the sea of forgetfulness, you will be no different from those who made 'pebble mistakes.' You can reclaim your life and start over; bounce back and pursue your dream life.

"You are now free to go.
"The choice is yours.
"It always is.
"What shall become of your dreams?"

Chapter 5

THE FLIPSIDE OF LOVE

"This was not just another example of office politics. Some aspects of this were pure evil. And nothing justifies those who allowed it to be amplified. Therein lay my confidence.

"God won't be God if He let that pass without intervening."

The Flipside of Love

We have already established that relationships

make life worthwhile. God invented relationships. Family is wonderful. Friends help give meaning to life. Loving someone, and someone loving you, is magical. The whole concept of social media is largely based on the principle of relationships and the human need for relationships. We all look for the number of likes and comments on our posts, we even get excited if we manage to create a viral moment. That is perhaps why social media has changed the world – the need for relationships, to be connected to other people.

However, as every adult has come to understand, not all people are loving and caring; not all people we meet will display integrity, have compassion, or embrace a sense of fair play. There are mean people. There are selfish people. There are manipulators. There are narcissists. There are disturbed people. And some are, well, evil.

When we interact with people like these, we can get very disappointed. It can be a spousal relationship, a relative, a boss on the job, a coworker, or a business partner. It can also be a person in a position of trust such as a policeman, attorney, judge, or other people who, in the exercise of the responsibilities of their positions, have a major impact on other people's lives.

One of the main reasons people get discouraged and give up on their dreams is because of traumatic experiences with bad people; people we sometimes call toxic people. The words and actions of toxic people can deeply hurt, undermine, and obstruct our progress. They make simple things complicated. They get some type of perverse satisfaction by seeing others hurt or fail. They are dream killers.

In the pursuit of our dreams, none of us is likely to escape encountering one or more of these toxic people. Many of us have been demoralized and driven to walk away because of wounds caused by haters. They can leave us dazed and emotionally wounded and without the will to fight. So we live broken, in a "what-if" world, wondering what could have been if it were not for the dream killers we came across. But even in the most extreme cases of roadblocks put up by people who like to see others fail, your dream can still flourish. It is a truth that God can take the things that were meant to harm you and turn them into things that prosper you.

When God Intervenes

Study this true story. It has all the elements of being knocked down by unfair, perhaps corrupt, behaviour, but God comes through to give a huge bounce back in the end. And the perpetrators – well, read on.

I came from very a humble family background. I grew up in poverty. My parents struggled so that I would be educated. And

The Flipside of Love

this education opened doors for me to change my circumstances and not live in poverty. I got a job in a well-respected field and worked very hard to develop a career.

I used the sound background of ethics and principles that were taught to me by my parents, particularly my father, to guide my life. Over the years I worked my way up to a very senior position in the company. Mine was a story of success and overcoming serious odds to build a career.

I did additional studies while working and I was blessed to eventually earn post-graduate qualifications. From feedback and other appraisals over the years, I was considered to be articulate and I stood out in some ways as a mentor and leader in my area of the business. I had a sense of humour. I was a champion for professionalism and ethical conduct. I had a wonderful family. It took me years of hard work, studies and long hours of work to get to the senior position that I was in. I was living my best life. Through it all, I tried to be a regular person, without arrogance or aloofness. My desire was always to use my success to make others succeed.

Then suddenly life changed. Everything turned upside down.

A new employee came to the department that I managed. She asked to see me a few times to get career advice. Eventually, I heard conversations in the informal network that she was saying

What Shall We Become of Your Dreams

that she had been a victim of serious crimes before she came to the company. Later, she would tell the same stories to me.

The story she told was a bizarre story of the worst type of crime one could experience. She wanted to know if those experiences would affect her continued employment with the company. As usual, I gave the best advice I could, tried to be supportive by listening, and asked those with whom she had shared her story to be as supportive as they could. Some of us tried to cheer her up.

As time progressed, I made certain observations and got feedback about different comments that the young lady was making, and I became concerned about whether the stories she told were fabricated; none of it appeared to be true. I was not sure, but I became concerned that if something was indeed wrong, it could be indicative of a personality that would constitute a risk to the staff and the company. I planned to discuss with Human Resources how we could intervene and provide help, if it turned out that help was needed.

Somehow she realized I was planning to seek advice about her stories and utterances. She appeared intimidated by it, and she retaliated. She became concerned about losing her job. She sent a message to me, "Keep your mouth shut, or I will create a big stink!"

I did not consider that a professional worth his salt could be si-

The Flipside of Love

lenced by a threat like that, so I ignored it and went to my senior manager about it. And the threat was carried out.

She made a series of serious allegations against me. Speaking generally, 99.9% of the charges were fabricated and the .1% truth was used in such a context to make all the untruths look credible. One senior executive seized upon the development and acted like an overzealous prosecutor. She went after me, and in my opinion, breached all kinds of professional ethics and rules of fairness. The basis of the allegations was telephone calls I was accused of making from a company cell phone and a lighthearted text message that was intended to be supportive based on the story of trauma she told me and others.

Since the company owned the phone, and I was certain that all the allegations about phone calls were false, I pleaded with the "prosecutor" to authorize access to the phone records for a detailed analysis of the call log relative to the accusations. I was ignored. I pleaded for a polygraph assessment (lie detector test). I was ignored. I even suggested a psychological evaluation to allow a psychologist to "get inside my head" to know if I was lying. I was ignored with that too.

There appeared to be a deliberate avoidance of objective, verifiable, or scientific analysis of the allegations.

The "prosecutor" was very disrespectful, at times shouting at me. She refused to listen to neutral people who tried to warn her that the allegations against me may be part of a conspiracy.

She took decisions that were designed to humiliate me. Even tiny, trivial, and insignificant things and some random acts of kindness were mischaracterized to look like something nefarious on my part.

She threatened to leak the matter to the media to scandalize me, claiming that she had ways to handle the media. I will always remember where I sat in the room on the executive floor when she put her fingers next to her ears and mouth like we do to represent making a call, and said, "How would you like the phone to wake you up first thing in the morning with someone on the other end asking, 'Have you seen the front page of the newspaper?'" I presumed she made that threat because she was aware of my strong pride in my values and because some members of my family were public figures.

So my initial concern about a potential risk to the staff and the company disappeared, and a panel was constituted to investigate charges against me! Plot twist! It was comparable to going to the police to report a robbery, and you get charged for robbing the robber.

The "prosecutor" put together a panel that was headed by a women's rights activist. No, I am not being facetious. That was

The Flipside of Love

the standard of fairness used. But I had little concern about all of this for several reasons. The charges could have been so easily disproved by objective evidence and because one of my life's philosophies was that I would be more concerned about the truth that I cannot defend, than a lie. But more importantly, I spent all my adult life believing in God and the power of name of Jesus. I have recommended Him to countless people, and I have seen Him come through for me countless times. I didn't think He would fail me this time.

My perspective was that whereas truth told about me that I can't defend might be my problem to solve, lies told about me is God's problem to solve.

So despite the bizarre turn of events, I was calm. I went through the process. The activist head of the investigation panel misled me on a key aspect of the proceedings that undermined my ability to defend myself.

Ultimately, they found no evidence to support the allegations against me. But they did make a tangential comment about "inappropriateness." I was never told what was inappropriate. I was not called to make a defense of inappropriateness. To this day, I have no idea what they were referring to.

From the inception, I warned the company that they were on a wild goose chase. I tried to tell them that the young lady was not

What Shall We Become of Your Dreams

a bad person, she just needed help and that she was being misled by more experienced persons who had grouses. I had no animosity then, and I don't have any now. I tried to impress upon them that it was part of our responsibility as a company to assist staff who appeared to need guidance. But they won't listen. I believe if they had listened, the young lady may have been a successful young professional today.

When it was all done, a top executive of the company asked me if I wanted to quit my job because of all the drama. He hinted at some sort of arrangement. But I refused. I looked him in the eye and I said, "There are several examples in the Bible of people who had similar experiences as I had, and God vindicated them." It was like Nehemiah said, "Why should such a man as I flee?"[8]

So I left the office that day, saying to myself, "Okay, Holy Spirit, it's your turn now. Do your thing." I was knocked down harder than many men would ever be knocked down. But I waited on my sponge ball moment. With prayer. With fasting. With faith. With Jesus.

Was I a perfect senior manager? No. Did I make mistakes? Yes. Did I sometimes make a bad decision? Yes. Did I learn lessons from this ordeal? Certainly.

But nothing justifies the awful lies. This was not just another example of office politics. Some aspects of this were pure evil per-

8 Nehemiah 6:11 KJV

petuated by those who should know better. And nothing justifies those who allowed it to be amplified. Therein lay my confidence. God wouldn't be God if He let that pass without intervening.

Can't Keep a Blessed Man Down

After the whole ordeal ended, things were never the same for me on the job. But there was one thing that was still the same: my confidence in God. I didn't waver. Then just over a year after that, I got an offer for which I did not apply. It was to be the chief executive of the local subsidiary of a large international company with operations in seven countries. I accepted. My salary was forty percent more than I was making. I was now at the top in my chosen field. I felt like David: "...you prepare a table before me in the presence of my enemies."[9] That was my sponge ball moment. I was knocked down hard, but I bounced back higher. My confidence in the Lord Jesus Christ was not misplaced.

When it seems as if your dream is dead, there is Jesus. He has experience in resurrecting things! If you haven't yet partnered with Him, you had better do it now.

But God wasn't done. I was a lot wiser and more cautious, but I brought my same values to this new job: people-centeredness, integrity, fairness, humility, commitment to excellence, mentorship, among others.

---

9 Psalm 23:5 NIV

What Shall We Become of Your Dreams

After just one year, I was winning The Group's top awards. The country I was managing became the best-performing country in The Group. We were breaking record after record. I had a wonderful team, and we were making magic.

After almost ten amazing years, I left that job, and using several key measures, my country grew to more than twice the size it was when I started, and it was still the best performing among all the countries in The Group.

Boomerang

You will recall that I mentioned earlier how a senior member of the executive cast herself in the role of prosecutor and relentlessly went after me. Recall how she threatened to scandalize me by leaking the allegations to the media.

There were three key individuals in the conspiracy against me: the person making the allegations, the "prosecutor executive" who threatened the media leak, and the person to whom she reported, her boss. Even though the boss himself was respectful and supportive throughout, he failed to restrain her even though I told him everything, and therefore he was spiritually accountable for the conduct he did nothing to stop. Remember her threat, "How would you like the phone to wake you up first thing in the morning with someone on the other end asking, 'Have you seen the front page of the newspaper?'"

The Flipside of Love

Well, within a few months, all three of them ended up in the front page headlines of the most widely circulated newspapers in the country. And all the stories were either scandalous or very tragic. The "prosecutor" who threatened me became a central figure in the biggest scandal to ever hit the company in its over twenty-five-year history. The story dominated the news for months.

These two senior executives in my story – one who had moved on to another entity – were the people who had the power to prevent a series of injustices but did not. Both of them ended up being accused of, implicated in, or responsible for things like fraud, duplicity, incompetence, insider-trading, lying, and different flavors of corruption or dishonesty. Regulators got involved. The police got involved. There were calls for criminal investigations and criminal charges. And all of it played out on the front pages and in lead stories in national newspapers and on television, in the full glare of the world. Exactly what one of them threatened to do to me.

Now consider what the Word of God says about conduct such as theirs. In Galatians Chapter 6, "Don't be misled; you cannot mock the justice of God. You will always reap what you sow."[10]

And in Psalm 7, "They dig a deep pit to trap others, then fall in it themselves. The trouble they make for others backfires on them. The violence they plan falls on their own heads."[11]

---

10 *Galatians 6:7 NLT*
11 *Psalm 7:15-16 NLT*

What Shall We Become of Your Dreams

If among the three key persons in this conspiracy, one of them ended up in front page headlines, you may conclude that it was a coincidence. If two of them ended up in the headlines, you may pause and wonder. But all three? That was not coincidence. That was a classic case of spiritual consequences.

I still believe that certain individuals, primarily the "prosecutor", failed the young lady because they did not give her the help she needed. I still believe that if those persons who failed both of us haven't repented, they and their future generations will continue to deal with the spiritual consequences of that injustice.

From my experience, many professionals tend to separate their conduct in the office from their conduct in the rest of their lives. They tend not to see God as having a role in the workplace, so they do not associate what they do as professionals with activities that are sinful or offensive to God. But all conduct has spiritual consequences, and those who deliberately engage in nasty office politics should know that it is offensive God. The attempt to disguise dishonesty, lying, or corruption as office politics, thinking that they will escape the notice of God, is extremely misguided.

The executives who got embroiled in all these front-page scandals were probably innocent.

The Flipside of Love

But so was I.

They reaped what they sowed.

God hates the hands that shed innocent blood.[12]

Always do the right thing.

---

12 Proverbs 6:17 KJV

Chapter 6

A ROCKY ROAD

"One of the things that is responsible for broken dreams is feeling like a failure; the feeling that 'this cannot be God's will' since so many things are going wrong."

A Rocky Road

Exodus 13 tells an interesting story about when God was leading the people of Israel out of slavery from Egypt and taking them to the Promised Land. It says, "God did not lead them along the main road that runs through the Philistine territory even though that was the shortest route to the Promised Land. God led them in a longer, roundabout way through the wilderness toward the Red Sea."[13] Now, why would God make it harder for them to get to their dream? Surely, God should make things easier, not more difficult.

But God had good reasons. The chapter goes on to explain that if they had gone through the geographically shorter route, they would have encountered many enemies and faced many battles. These obstacles would have demoralized them and caused them to want to go back to Egypt; to give up on their dream.

However, through the longer route, without attacks from enemies, they went forward through a less hazardous journey with extreme confidence.

How many times we must have complained about the road that God is taking us without realizing that He had a plan to take us safely to our dream. Who among us hasn't asked, "Lord, why is this taking so long? Why is this so hard? When will end?" The road to a dream is hardly ever smooth. It is a rocky road with many twists and turns, many obstacles and challenges, but

---

13 Exodus 13:17-18 NLT

What Shall We Become of Your Dreams

through it all, God directs us through the safest path. He sees ahead. He knows our strengths, weaknesses, and limitations. And He guides us along the best path even though it does not always fit our rational thinking.

This is why our confidence must always be in what the book of Romans says: "And we know that God causes everything to work together for the good of those who love him; those who are called according to his purpose for them."[14]

The book of Genesis tells us the story of Joseph. God had given him dreams of greatness. But his dreams attracted intense envy from his siblings, and they plotted to destroy him. Their plots caused Joseph to go through a series of very difficult experiences. The initial plan was to kill him. I am going to rephrase this story as a conversation between God and Joseph.

Joseph: "God, why did they have to throw me into that horrible pit? That was a very horrible experience. I could have died in there."

God: "Joseph, you didn't realize, but when those guys threw you in the pit, they actually intended to kill you. That was the plan. They had it all worked out. They didn't know it, but they couldn't kill you because you had a dream to fulfil."

Joseph: "I was so happy when they took me out. But then they

---

14 Romans 8:28 NLT

A Rocky Road

sold me to slave traders! From a pit to a slave is not much of an improvement."

God: "You see Joseph, when the slave traders were passing by, instead of killing you, the guys sold you to the traders. Being sold to slave traders was a horrible thing. But it saved your life. Being sold was better than being dead because if they killed you, they would have killed your dream too."

Joseph: "And did they have to sell me to a foreign land? Egypt! So far away from my family, even if I managed to escape, where would I go?"

God: "Okay, so the traders took you to Egypt where they sold you to Potiphar. It was humiliating to be sold. It stripped you of your dignity. You felt like a piece of property or some type of animal. But your dream was to be fulfilled in Egypt, and Potiphar was a very powerful man in Egypt who was close to Pharaoh. Pharaoh was key to your dreams. And Potiphar was your link to Pharaoh."

Joseph: "Then while serving Potiphar, I thought I was finally settled. I saw that You were blessing me, even though I was a slave. And then out of the blue, that woman framed me, and I ended up in jail!"

God: "I know, as if everything else wasn't enough, while you were blessed and very successful serving Potiphar, you were

What Shall We Become of Your Dreams

falsely accused and imprisoned. It would have been very painful to be framed and imprisoned after you did the right thing. But your stint in prison also held a key to your dreams.

"It was in jail you interpreted dreams for a man who, when he was released, told Pharaoh how gifted you were at interpreting dreams. That is how you were released and taken to Pharaoh to interpret his dreams.

"And your inspired interpretation of Pharaoh's dreams led directly to you fulfilling your own dream; the same dream that I put in your heart a long time before.

"So while it was a long rocky road, every step took you closer to your dream, because a dream never dies. You went through the four stages of a dream: birth, journey, struggle, and achievement. You lived your best life. You saved lives. I'm sure you are satisfied with how it all ended.

"Let your life story be a lesson to other dreamers. The road to a dream is hardly ever smooth sailing. There is envy. There is hate. There are lies. There is unfairness. There is pain. There is discouragement. But if the Lord your God is directing your dream, you will get there. And in the end, that is what matters, isn't it?"

Indeed, there are lessons for dreamers. How many dreams die just when the journey is starting because the road gets rough?

A Rocky Road

It is said that when you feel like quitting, remember why you started in the first place. You must remember the birth of the dream; why it was birthed, where it was birthed, what you saw in your future at the time of birth. You must have had a picture of the final product in your heart. You saw a vision of yourself at Stage Four of the dream and it looked wonderful. That is why you started in the first place.

Take an example from Jesus. At the birth of His dream, it was picture-perfect. He was growing in wisdom and stature, in favor with God and man. As a young child, He had an IQ beyond His age. He was in the temple debating with scholars who were much older and more qualified than Himself. If that were your son, you would be a proud parent.

He started out as an incredible child. He ended up fulfilling His dream and taking a seat at the right hand of the Father in heaven, with a name that is above every other name; the most powerful name in heaven, in the earth and even under the earth.

Seems like a dream life. But that's when you go from Stage One directly to Stage Four. The stages in-between are not so exciting.

During Stages Two and Three, He was hated. He was vilified. They told lies about Him. They plotted to kill Him. They called Him names. He was betrayed. A criminal was preferred to Him. He was beaten. He was humiliated. He was crucified. But

What Shall We Become of Your Dreams

through it all, He was still on the road to His dream.

He was knocked down hard at Calvary. I could imagine His enemies saying, "Let us see what shall become of His dreams." But when He bounced back via the resurrection, He bounced back as high as heaven. This was perhaps the hardest knock-down in history. And also the highest bounce-back of all time. It is a classic demonstration of "the harder you get knocked down, the higher you bounce back."

Hear the Whole Story

We generally see the people who inspire us when they are at Stage Four. We hardly ever see them at the birth stage, and therefore we could have a limited understanding of what it takes to get to Stage Four. This can create a misleading view of how a dream comes to pass.

If I tell you that I moved from poverty to a clerical level in an organization – just helping out with miscellaneous duties – to a top position in my chosen career, that would seem like a fairy tale life. That is because it takes you from Stage One to Stage Four without an appreciation of what happens in-between. And that is misleading.

To properly understand how a dream comes true, I have to tell you about the mistakes, the errors in judgment, the discrimina-

A Rocky Road

tion, the times I was in the doghouse, the time when I was demoted, the time I was fired, the years of studying to improve my qualifications, the hundreds of hours in training, the time I was falsely accused, the attempts to tarnish my reputation, the times I was stabbed in the back, and on and on.

When you understand all the stages, then you can properly understand your own pursuit. And you will not get sidetracked when things look like a disaster. Go back to earlier in this chapter and read the conversation between God and Joseph as paraphrased from the Book of Genesis. And you will appreciate the full picture.

One of the things that is responsible for broken dreams is feeling like a failure; the feeling that "this cannot be God's will" since so many things are going wrong. If you are blessed and walking honestly before God, you are not blessed sometimes. Being blessed is not like a Christmas light that goes on and off. In whatever state you find yourself, you are still blessed. Joseph was blessed when he was a slave and blessed when he was a prisoner.

Look at this account of a part of the life of the Apostle Paul from Acts 28: "Publius's father was ill with a fever and dysentery, and Paul went in and prayed for him, and laying hands on him, he healed him. Then all the other sick people on the island came and were healed."[15] That was a powerful demonstration of

---

15 *Acts 28:8-9 NLT*

What Shall We Become of Your Dreams

the gifts of God operating in Paul's life. I can't think of a real servant of Christ who would not like to be able to do that. But at that time Paul was a prisoner. He didn't stop being blessed because he was going through a difficult season of life. Neither was his dream lost.

This is what God said to Joshua: "Moses my servant is dead. Therefore, the time has come for you to lead these people into the land I have given them. I promise you what I promised Moses. Wherever you set foot, you will be on land I have given you. No one will be able to stand against you as long as you live. I will be with you as I was with Moses. I will not fail you or abandon you."[16]

There are few words of God more clear and direct than those spoken to Joshua. Imagine this, "No one will be able to stand against you as long as you live." But God was not done yet. God went on to say, "Be strong and very courageous. Be careful to obey all the instructions that Moses gave you. This is my command, be strong and courageous. Do not be afraid or discouraged."[17]

Even though God gave Joshua some of the most powerful and unambiguous promises ever given to anyone, God went on to emphasize over and over that he must be strong and very courageous. Why does he need to be very courageous if God is being

16 *Joshua 1:2-5 NLT*
17 *Joshua 1:7-9 NLT*

A Rocky Road

very blunt and specific to him, "I will not fail you or abandon you"?

Why? Because the pursuit of a dream can get tough.

Very tough.

Even for those who are blessed and called by God.

Even when God has got your back.

Chapter 7

STARTING OVER

"There are many before you who started all over again and found outstanding success the second time. The bounce-back was so amazing that it was worth every moment of the second time."

Starting Over

My favorite type of secular music is love
songs. I have been a fan of love songs for as long as I can remember, certainly from my teenage days. During my teenage school days, I often challenged my friends to turn on the radio at any time, and chances were I'd be able to tell them the name of the song that was playing and the singer. I was actually an amateur DJ at one time. Turning pro was a teenage fantasy. But I shelved that for other pursuits as I matured. I concluded that DJ-ing was a hobby, not a career.

And as I was writing this book, an old classic love song from the 70s came to mind. It is such a popular favorite that it has been covered by several artists over the years. It's a good make-up song. It tells how hard it is to start all over again. Look it up. Part of the lyrics go like this:

Starting all over again is going to be rough
We lost what we had
That's what hurt us so bad
Set us back a thousand years
But we gonna make it up
Though I know it's gonna be tough
To erase the hurt and fears
Starting all over again is going to be hard
But I pray to the Lord, to help us make it[18]

As we know, art imitates life. Love songs are written to reflect

---

18 Mel & Tim, Starting All Over Again, Stax Records, 1972

What Shall We Become of Your Dreams

real life scenarios so that a large cross-section of the population can identify with the lyrics and listen, enjoy, and pay to acquire the songs. Therefore, one can conclude that, in addition to its music, melody, and rendition, the lyrics of a hit love song capture sentiments with which a lot of people can identify.

It is true. Starting all over again is tough. Not just with relationships but with any dream that was dear to your heart. Starting over makes you think of what you consider as wasted years. You reflect on all the time, effort, money, pains, and struggles, and it's heartbreaking to contemplate living it all over again. You look at the fragments of what used to be your hard work – what represented your dream – and the memories hurt. Really hurt. You feel like you are going backward. And going backward is not a good feeling.

You used to get up early in the morning, you radiated a unique kind of energy as you went through the day. Your dream was pushing you.

Now, with the daunting prospect of having to start over, you lie down a lot. It's a big effort to muster enthusiasm to do anything. You watch television a lot. You watch movie series after movie series. You spend hours on social media, going through everything in your feed; liking, commenting, and posting sometimes. Your rhythm has slowed as you ponder, "What shall become of my dreams?"

Here's some hope. You are not the first. You will not be the last. There are many before you who started all over again and found outstanding success the second time. The bounce-back was so amazing that it was worth every moment of the second time.

Reflect on this excerpt from the book of Jeremiah: "Here's another message from the Lord. Go down to the shop where clay pots and jars are made and I will talk to you there. I did as he told me and found a potter working at his wheel. But when the vessel he was forming did not turn out as he wished, he kneaded it into a lump and started again."[19]

The potter is a representation of our lives. And the vessel that the potter was making represents our dreams. When a dream falls apart, we have two choices: start over or quit, give up, and throw in the towel. How we view our "failure" will determine what choice we make.

The Best Teachers

If I ask you to name one or two of the best teachers you have ever had, what names would come to mind? Take a moment and think about it before you continue. You are likely to be among the majority of people in the world if you reflected on a teacher you had during your formal schooling. School teachers are among the most influential people in our lives. I believe every-

---

19 Jeremiah 18:1-4 LB

What Shall We Become of Your Dreams

body has a fond memory of at least one teacher. Teaching is one of the world's most noble professions, although society tends to glamorize many others more than teachers; doctors, lawyers, movie stars, rock stars, etc. Teachers are in many ways like parents – everybody has one or had one.

Here's the thing. The teachers we are so thankful for are the teachers from the classroom at school. How about if we expand the definition of teachers to include any person or experience that has taught us a valuable life lesson?

Back to the example of the potter. When the vessel we are forming – the dream we are pursuing – doesn't come out the way we had hoped it would, we must go back and start over. But we must not go back and do the same thing all over again without first consulting the teachers. What lessons were there to learn? Is there something we did wrong the first time? Did we not plan properly? Did we trust the wrong people? Were we too impatient? Did somebody undermine our efforts? Did we not take time to develop the personal attributes required such as skills, training, knowledge?

The answers to all of those questions were teachers. And we should value them. That person who betrayed you was a teacher. The person who undermined your dream was a teacher. That divorce you went through was a teacher. The bad people you met were teachers too. These were all teachers because we learn

Starting Over

from every experience, and if we carefully review every one of them, there will be valuable lessons to learn as we go for our bounce-back moment.

In my professional life, I learned a lot from the "bad people" with whom I worked. When I faced unfairness, I learned not to be unfair because I can empathize with the pain of unfairness. When I was falsely accused and given a raw deal, I learned not to rush to judgment and to properly consider all the facts. When I saw others pretend to be impartial but they had already formed predetermined opinions, I learned to assess situations based on the merits of the evidence before coming to conclusions.

The takeaway is this: some teachers teach you what to do, while others teach what not to do. Some experiences teach us what works and should be repeated; others teach us what did not work and should not be repeated.

So when, like the potter, things don't work the first time, if we see the experiences as teachers, we tend to appreciate them instead of letting them get us discouraged or bitter.

That is the essence of "experience" that employers seek. Experience teaches us skills, improves our know-how, and enhances our competence. And experience has a lot of learning moments disguised as mistakes, disappointments or pain. Learning can be described as a series of errors and corrections.

What Shall We Become of Your Dreams

In the study of management, there is a popular story about the approach of a hugely successful businessman who was asked if he is going to fire an employee who had made a mistake that cost the company hundreds of thousands of dollars. The boss replied that he was not going to fire the employee because he had invested a huge amount of money training him. His rationale was that if he fired him, another company would hire him and benefit from the experience and the knowledge that was gained from the mistake. He considered that cost of the employee's mistake to be a "payment" to train him.

Clearly, that businessman had an understanding of what a teacher is. The mistake was a teacher who was paid a six-figure "teaching salary," and he wasn't going to let the input of that teacher go to waste. A lot of trauma was avoided by the redefinition of teaching and learning in that story. Imagine the painful experience that the person who made the mistake would have gone through if he was fired. Thankfully, his mistake was a teacher, and the boss was a wise school principal. We too can avoid trauma in our personal and professional lives, as well as in the pursuit of our dreams, if we broaden our understanding of who or what is a teacher.

However, if we are to learn lessons that would help serve as springboards for our bounce-back, we must be very honest with

Starting Over

ourselves. We have to know how to look at ourselves objectively. It's very challenging to objectively assess oneself. If we don't do this well, we will only focus all our attention on people or circumstances outside of ourselves and important lessons will be lost.

In their book, *If Those Who Reach Could Touch*, Gail and Gordon MacDonald write:

> It is one thing to avoid transparency when dealing with others. It is an even more serious matter when we slowly become less transparent to ourselves. As we noted before, this can be called self-deceit. Unable to face some truths about a part of our lives, we begin to suppress it, shading it over so that we don't have to keep facing the same pain. The covering over can be done by lying to ourselves, blaming the event upon someone else, remaking the actual history into a story that is most suitable to our pride. Before long, we have created a form of personal propaganda, which we not only share with others but come to believe ourselves.[20]

Among all the teachers you encounter, be a teacher to yourself.

We can draw inspiration from a lot of very famous people we view as successes; people who had teachable moments that were not from traditional classroom teachers. A number of peo-

20 Gail and Gordon MacDonald, If Those Who Reach Could Touch, New Jersey, Fleming H Revell, 1984, Page 33

What Shall We Become of Your Dreams

ple whose names have become synonymous with excellence or success throughout the world have had moments that looked like failures. They had to learn the lessons life was teaching them and still go after their dreams.

Walt Disney was reportedly fired from the *Kansas City Star* because he lacked imagination.

Oprah Winfrey was fired from her job as a TV anchor in Baltimore for being too emotionally invested in her stories.

Henry Ford failed multiple times prior to succeeding with Ford.

And Steven Spielberg was twice rejected by a Cinematic Arts School.

What if they had not decided to start over, to bounce back? What if they had not learned the lessons from the teachers outside the classroom?

All of Jesus' disciples were failures in different ways and at different times. They slept during prayer time. They selfishly sought positions of influence. They chased children away. They had little faith at times. They had no faith at other times. They wanted to burn-up people with whom they had a dispute. They failed to keep promises. They broke up other people's services who were not in their group. They abandoned Jesus. They went back to their old lives. Peter cursed and lied.

Starting Over

David was a failure at one time. Moses was a failure at one time.

But they all bounced back.

They all became successful after they failed.

Except for Judas.

And you are not Judas.

Chapter 8

JUST RELEASE IT

"Too many of us spend too much of our days and nights consuming negative energy, often in some sort of fight, being angry with something or someone. This mindset, sometimes referred to as a 'negativity bias,' is bad for our mental health and will not lead to success."

Cher's true story is similar to many others in her country at that time. There was tension in the family when she wanted a mixed marriage; not mixed race, but mixed religion. They eventually overcame that hurdle and got married. Then she had a son who tragically lost his life to a scorpion's sting. She later had a daughter. Their lives had settled down. Through it all, Cher also struggled with her faith, abandoning it sometimes and going back to it at other times

From all appearances, they had a happy marriage. Then one day, as many people do, her husband left for New York to find work, hoping to secure a better life for his wife and daughter. While he was in New York, they kept in contact by telephone; a long-distance relationship, you might say. Eventually, the calls got fewer and fewer, especially the calls coming from the husband in New York. Cher began to suspect that something was happening; she perceived that something was going wrong with her marriage. Her husband was different.

Then one of his rare telephone calls delivered news that made the suspicion even worse.

"My line of work is running out," he said, "and to cut cost, I'll be moving in with a friend. I will not have a telephone, and it seems as if I have to get married here to get my papers in order. I wouldn't be seeing you and my daughter for about five years." This was more evidence to Cher that something was wrong.

What Shall We Become of Your Dreams

Some weeks after, she received another phone call. This time her husband had an announcement to make. He said that he "had somebody" and would not be returning home.

"One night at a party I met someone and after a series of events, I moved in with her. She is giving me everything that I wanted, and we are happy together," he said.

Cher was devastated. To make things worse, the "somebody else" with whom he had moved in kept calling her. Some of the calls were threatening, some were contemptuous, but all were ill-mannered and rude.

Cher restored her spiritual life. She came to the church where I attended and got support and advice from us. She fasted and prayed. After a few weeks, she suddenly got a call from her husband. He wanted to come back home. Cher bought a travel ticket and sent it to him. She met him at the airport and drove him home. When he arrived home, Cher had his favorite meal waiting for him. The marriage was restored, and eventually they were once again enjoying marital bliss.

And here is the main point of this true story. Cher never once questioned her husband about what happened in New York. It wasn't Las Vegas, but what happened in New York stayed in New York. She never accused him. She never reminded him of his past – his past sins, you might say. They both renewed their faith, and she just forgave him, took up from where they left off, and moved on.

There is a lesson in this story about answered prayer. To get her family back, Cher restored her faith, fasted, prayed, and got advice from her church. But in this chapter, I want to focus on another lesson: the ability to forgive; to release the deepest hurts that we have suffered and bounce back to reclaim our dreams. I don't know how many people in a similar situation would be able to handle themselves as the wife did in this story.

I knew this couple personally. And the husband said that one of the main reasons that they were able to return to marital happiness is because his wife did not bring up the past or pester him about it. From my perspective, I think that another reason for the happiness was because he remained faithful and committed to the marriage. If he had displayed similar disregard for his marriage, it wasn't going to work.

One of the things that I have observed in the church, as well as in corporate life and in politics, is how often we passionately repeat the highest principles, but when confronted with real-life scenarios, the principles are abandoned for expediency; for the less noble side of human behavior. What a beautiful world it would be if all the people who speak – or preach – about integrity, forgiveness, transparency, fairness, etc., actually practice these principles. Cher's story is one where somebody actually

What Shall We Become of Your Dreams

practiced the principles that her faith teaches.

Most people know the story of the Prodigal Son in which the father received him back home without chastising him about his past. We know that Peter seemed quite pleased with himself to ask Jesus if forgiving someone seven times is a good yardstick. We know that Jesus shocked him by telling him he was way short; it's more like seventy times seven. Jesus set such a high bar that the disciples' response was, "Lord, increase our faith!"[21]

Despite the very clear teachings of Jesus that millions claim to believe, many dreams are lost because the dreamers get so emotionally burdened by past betrayal, failures, grudges, and bitterness that they are unable to muster the strength to pick up the pieces and move on.

More Than Religion

Achieving dreams takes strength of character. And to develop or maintain that strength, we have to work on our minds, our thought life. If we load ourselves with negativity, we will drain our emotional energy and be unable to fight for our dreams.

The value of forgiveness is not only something you hear about in church. There are several intervention studies on the subject by various non-religious researchers.

---

21 Luke 17:5 KJV

Just Release It

Stanford University is the home of one of the largest intervention studies on the training of interpersonal forgiveness: *Effects of a Group Forgiveness Intervention on Forgiveness, Perceived Stress, and Trait-Anger.*[22] It is called the Stanford Forgiveness Project, and it trained a group of adults in forgiveness and observed their responses to it. The study tested five hypotheses. In these hypotheses "target transgression" refers the person or source of the issue, hurt, or pain that necessitated the need for forgiveness.

Hypothesis 1: *The training will reduce negative thoughts and emotions with respect to the target transgression.*

Hypothesis 2: *The training will increase positive emotions and perspectives with respect to the target transgression.*

Hypothesis 3: *The training will increase confidence to perform specific forgiveness-related actions with respect to the target transgression.*

Hypothesis 4: *The training will promote forgiveness and reduce offense-taking for events other than the specific event that brought the person into the study.*

Hypothesis 5: *The training will produce improvements in perceived stress and trait anger.*

---

22 Harris, Alex H. S, et al, 2001

What Shall We Become of Your Dreams

Ultimately, the researchers noted, "Implications are considerable, including the possibility that skills-based forgiveness training may prove effective in reducing anger as a coping style, reducing perceived stress and physical health symptoms, and thereby may help reduce allostatic load (e.g., immune and cardiovascular functioning) in daily living."[23]

The Bible is not just a "religious book"; it is a book about life. It trains us how to live successful, healthy, and purposeful lives. One of my favorite bits of guidance is in the book of Philippians, where it says, "Finally, whatsoever things are true, whatsoever things are honest, whatsoever things are just, whatsoever things are pure, whatsoever things are lovely, whatsoever things are good, whatsoever things are praiseworthy, think on these things."[24]

Too many of us spend too much of our days and nights consuming negative energy; often in some sort of fight, telling stories of things that upset us, being angry with something or someone, or seeing all the bad things in our world. This mindset, sometimes referred to as a "negativity bias," is bad for our mental health and will not lead to success.

The lesson from that quote from the book of Philippians is an encouragement to fill our minds with positive, healthy thoughts. The benefits of positive thoughts are supported by modern-day

23 Harris, Alex H. S, et al, 2001
24 Philippians 4:8 KJV

research. Several studies by recognized medical and scientific experts have validated the impact of our thoughts and emotions on our lives — our behavior, relationships, and physical health. That is why is it so important for us be aware of the consequences of intense negative emotions and use that awareness to influence our thoughts and reactions to developments in our environments. Adjusting our emotional responses is not a straightforward matter. Managing emotions takes time, particularly if your emotional temperament is ingrained. You have to consciously train yourself to manage your emotions. It could also be achieved by professional help and or prayer. The Holy Spirit understands human emotions.

Prolonged stress from emotionally hostile stimuli, and the feelings that they generate, can affect our hormone stability and interfere with the part of the brain that influence happiness. All of these ultimately lead to a degradation in the quality of life and reduce the number of our days.

Medical research has also traced a number of health problems to the state of a person's mind. Things like frequent anger, deep disappointment, and feelings of failure, particularly if they are repressed or not treated, can cause a number of health conditions, including susceptibility to infection.

On the contrary, research has also shown that positivity and positive mindsets contribute to both a healthier physical life and greater happiness.

If we want to have a higher quality of life and enjoy the inner strength and self-confidence to pursue our dreams, it is vitally important to manage our emotions – our thought life, the things that dominate our thoughts.

This is correlated with what Jesus taught when He said that we must love our enemies and do good to those who have done us wrong. He wants us to move our focus away from the "negativity bias" which drains our emotional energy. He wants us to release the emotional weight that some of life's experiences impose on us.

Just release it.

In another place, Jesus said, "Do not worry about tomorrow, for tomorrow will bring its own worries. Today's trouble is enough for today."[25] I think He was guiding us away from taking on unnecessary stress by being preoccupied with things that we cannot control.

From Bitterness to Love

At one time, in my younger, less wise self, I was involved in a major conflict in my church. It was based on a disagreement about leadership style. It was so major that it did not appear that it would ever be resolved. It was very contentious. But after the anger and emotions settled, I reflected on the issues that led

---

25 Matthew 6:34 NLT

Just Release It

to the conflict, and I realized a lot of things: it was not as bad as I saw it at the time, it was blown out of proportion, it was as much, or more, my fault as it was anybody else's, and most importantly, if I did not want to be a hypocrite, I had to find a way to resolve it.

It's amazing how differently the mind sees things when one releases things like anger, bitterness, and unforgiveness. I could paraphrase Paula White-Cain, "Forgiveness is not erasing memory. It is memory without anger, revenge and bitterness."[26]

I still clearly remember the day in my living room when I was on my knees with tears in my eyes, and together with the other parties, the matter was resolved. Reconciliation took place, the negativity bias was released. And from then, it was moving forward.

And now more than twenty years after, I have been an advocate for conflict resolution and releasing emotional pain. It's almost never as bad as we think it is.

Pause. Reflect. Evaluate. With the help of the Holy Spirit.

There are many conflicts that are tearing families apart; very often conflicts arise over money, property, bills or inheritance. There is the story in the Book of Genesis[27] of Jacob stealing his brother's inheritance, as I choose to express it. When Esau realized that he was robbed by his brother Jacob, he broke down in

---

26 *Via Paula White-Cain's Twitter feed, June 2021*
27 *Genesis Chapter 27*

tears, and he begged to get back his inheritance, but it was too late. Then anger and bitterness took over. Esau hated his brother Jacob because of the stolen inheritance. "As soon as I am finished mourning for my father," Esau said, "I will find Jacob and kill him!"

That was extreme bitterness.

Sometime later, Jacob was told that Esau was coming his way with a contingent of 400 men. Jacob panicked, "With such an army he is coming to carry out his threat and kill me. He is going to kill my wife and children too!" Jacob implemented all sorts of tactics in anticipation of bloodshed. Eventually, they met face to face, and this was the scene: "Esau ran to meet Jacob and embraced him, threw his arms around his neck and kissed him and they both wept." There was a big happy family reunion of sorts; there were introductions all around, gifts were being exchanged and all manner of expressions of love were taking place. Jacob even said to Esau, "What a relief to see your friendly smile. It is like seeing the face of God!"

It's amazing how differently the mind sees things when one releases things like anger, bitterness, and unforgiveness.

Shake It Off and Move On

There are several examples and exhortations in the scriptures

Just Release It

about the importance of releasing the experiences that leave a bad taste in our mouths. Emotionally handcuffing ourselves to unpleasant feelings is a dream killer.

Even though Saul was a very imperfect king, Samuel had a long association with him. Samuel was the prophet who anointed him to be king at the start of his reign. However, there came a time when God had had enough of Saul's disobedience, and God decided that his reign must come to an end. God then told Samuel to inform Saul that his reign will be cut short. Samuel was very disturbed by that news. "Samuel was so deeply moved when he heard this, that he cried out to the Lord all night," 1 Samuel 15 tells us.[28]

Samuel continued to be distressed over Saul's rejection until God had to directly tell him to let it go. "You have mourned long enough for Saul. I have rejected him as king," God said to him. God then instructed Samuel to get up and get moving. There were other things Samuel had to do that would have been affected if he had not released the disappointment over Saul.

No matter how disappointed you are with a particular outcome, if you are to move forward, at some point you have to release the bad feelings and press on. The earlier the better. Otherwise, your life will stall and you will lose a lot of time, perhaps years, bemoaning the unfortunate developments.

---

28 1 Samuel 15:11 NLT

What Shall We Become of Your Dreams

Then there was the time when David's son was sick. David was extremely broken. He openly showed his pain and sorrow. This is how 2 Samuel 12 (NLT) describes it:

> David begged God to spare the child. He went without food and lay all night on the bare ground. The elders of his household pleaded with him to get up and eat, but he refused.
>
> Then on the seventh day, the child died. David's advisers were afraid to tell him. "He wouldn't listen to reason while the child was ill," they said. "What drastic thing will he do when we tell him the child is dead?"

It seems as if they thought David would commit suicide when he heard the news. But when he was told that the child died,

> David got up from the ground, washed himself, put on lotions, and changed his clothes. He went to the Tabernacle and worshiped the Lord. After that, he returned to the palace and was served food and ate.
>
> His advisers were amazed. "We don't understand you," they told him. "While the child was still living, you wept and refused to eat. But now that the child is dead, you have stopped your mourning and you are eating again."[29]

David explained to them that he asked God to spare the child but

---

29 *2 Samuel 12:20,21 NLT*

Just Release It

since that didn't happen, he accepted God's will and was ready to move on. There comes a time when we have to accept the will of the Lord and move on to the things that God still has for us to do. Otherwise, we will lose precious years brooding over things that cannot change while giving no attention to the things that we can change.

It is not a simple matter to conquer strong emotional distress and bounce back. These are not things that turn off instantly like using a switch. My intention is not to trivialize the deep wounds that we often suffer. Rather, I am challenging you not to lose yourself after you have lost something else or someone else. Whatever the source of your hurt, losing yourself over it only creates a bigger loss.

Even Jesus at one time told his disciples if they went to a house and the occupants of the house refused to welcome them, "Shake the dust off your feet and leave."[30]

Sometimes you just have to shake off an offence and move on. No quarrelling. No fighting. No hate. No bitterness. No melodrama. Whether it is the end of a relationship, quitting a job or leaving a church, just move on, minus the drama. Just release it.

---

30 *Matthew 10:14 NLT*

Things happen. Bad things.

We get hurt. Badly hurt.

We can forfeit the future by clinging to the pain of the past.

Or we can release the past.

Choose.

Chapter 9

BATTERED AND BRUISED BUT STILL A WINNER

"It is a mistake to dismiss a dream as too small unless one understands the value of that dream to the heart of the dreamer. It is unsafe to appoint ourselves as judges of another person's dreams."

Battered and Bruised but Still a Winner

Psychiatrist Victor E Frankl's *Man's Search for Meaning[31]* is described as one of the most influential books in America. Frankl was a survivor of the Nazi concentration and extermination camps in the early 1900s. His theory is that the primary human drive is the pursuit of what we find meaningful. It is a book about survival.

Frankl writes a lot about what kept many prisoners alive, and in many cases, it was a hope, an expectation of a better tomorrow, an expectation of a change in their circumstances:

> The prisoner who had lost faith in his future was doomed. With his loss of belief in the future, he also lost his spiritual hold; he let himself decline and became subject to mental and physical decay.

> The death rates in the week between Christmas 1944 and New Year's 1945 increased in the camp beyond all previous experience. The explanation for this increase did not lie in the harsh working conditions or the deterioration of our food supplies or a change of weather or epidemics. It was simply that the majority of the prisoners had lived in the naive hope that they would be home again by Christmas. As the time drew near and there was no encouraging news, the prisoners lost courage and disappointment overcame them. This had a dangerous influence on their

---

31 Viktor E Frankl, Man's Search for Meaning, Boston, Beacon Press, 2006, Page 76

What Shall We Become of Your Dreams

powers of resistance and a great number of them died.[32]

This is consistent with other literature about how the condition of the mind affects a person's will to live. It also speaks to the power of hope for tomorrow and the tragedy of the loss of hope. From my perspective, it is the power of a dream and the power of a determination to bounce back. Your dreams give you a purpose for living, a reason to fight and look forward to tomorrow. And when a dream is broken, we can become dispirited and lose our drive to move on. That is why it is so important to focus, not on the lost dream, but on the bounce-back moment in the future. This maintains your focus on the possibilities of the future and not on the trauma of the past.

Frankl quotes the German philosopher, Friedrich Nietzsche, "He who has a 'why' to live for can bear almost any 'how.'"[33] Your dream is your "why." You must know why you do what you do. Know why you are making the sacrifices. Know why you continue to push even when the odds appear to be against you. Know why you are burning the midnight oil. Know why you are foregoing some things now. Always know why. So when the going gets tough, you focus on the goal, on the endgame, on the why.

A dream doesn't necessarily mean an extraordinary accom-

32 *Viktor E Frankl, Man's Search for Meaning, Boston, Beacon Press, 2006, Page 76*
33 *Viktor E Frankl, Man's Search for Meaning, Boston, Beacon Press, 2006, Page 76*

plishment that's beyond the achievement of ordinary people. It doesn't have to be a once-in-a-lifetime achievement like an Olympic goal medal or something comparable to a superhero movie. It can be all that, but for most people, a dream is a lot simpler but no less impactful. Not everybody wants fame, fortune, publicity, or the adoration of a lot of people. Not everybody cares about being on the cover of a major magazine. Not everybody wants to own a million-dollar yacht to go sailing.

For those who are lonely, the big dream might simply be someone to love them or someone for them to love, or to get married and have a family. For others, it might be to have a child. It might be to own a home. Homeownership is a life goal of most young adults. It is one of those foundational dreams that sets up your adult life in a positive way. For others, it may be to land that dream job, or just to get a job; to get a promotion, to pass an examination, to own your dream car.

Dreams often match life. We dream of one thing when we are young and other things when we get older. Dreams also come in a hierarchy sometimes. You get the dream job. Then you want the dream house. Then you want the big promotion or you want to start a business. The bottom line is you must always know your dream and wake up every day with a plan. Do something every day that takes you closer to your dream.

Other dreams might be to serve God more effectively, to be

blessed with His gifts so that you are enabled to impact your church, your country or the world. You feel that there is a call in your heart to contribute in getting the message of Jesus to the world, or simply to your world. This is one of the noblest of dreams. But it has divine rules. You too must do something every day that takes you closer to your dream. You need to be clear that this is about selflessness, about service and sacrifice. You must be prepared to be a servant, to deny the flesh, to be submissive to authority, and to make yourself a vessel worthy to be used by the Holy Spirit.

This is true regardless of the type of dream you have for the kingdom of God. Whether it is prominent and visible or simply behind-the-scenes, the dream of service to God requires a pure heart and clean hands.

The Definition of Big

The value of a dream is in the heart of the dreamer. It is a mistake to dismiss a dream as too small unless one understands the value of that dream to the heart of the dreamer. It is unsafe to appoint ourselves as judges of another person's dreams. You have heard about love languages; well, we all have different dream languages. A big dream for one person is not necessarily a big dream for another person. Whereas the definition of "dream" is universal, the definition of "big" is unique to the dreamer.

The person who has had one long stable marriage and family may not be able to understand the heart of the people who gave everything they could have given to a relationship – love, commitment, time, money, blood, sweat and tears – and then lost it. There are millions of questions, there is loss of self-esteem or loss of self-confidence; there is the desire to forge a new relationship but the fear of a second failure hovers over the heart. To such people, there is no bigger dream than a chance to once again enjoy the beauty of a loving, stable relationship. Others may simply say, "Just move on with your life." But it's never that simple.

It is said that beauty lies in the eye of the beholder. Well, like beauty, dreams are in the eye of the beholder. And the hope of realizing that dream is what keeps the dreamer looking forward to a tomorrow.

Understanding Emotional Thresholds

Several years ago, I was the youth leader at one of the country's biggest churches. My youth group had more young people than the entire congregation of some churches. Working with this group was one of the most rewarding experiences of my life. The insights, guidance and support I was able to give to these young people helped shaped my outlook on serving people. I have seen many of them move on to lead very successful lives and ministries.

As is the norm among young people, two of them got into a relationship – courting or dating – as it is described. From all appearances, they had a good relationship. I was expecting a wedding invitation at any moment. Then things began to fall apart. Again, as is not unusual with young people, the young man in the relationship met someone else, and it appeared that his attention was diverted to another young woman. All three of them were in my youth group, so naturally I was asked to help clarify what was going on.

Eventually, the young man confirmed that he was no longer interested in the first relationship, and he was planning to marry the other girl. I did what I can to help the young lady who was heartbroken understand and move on. But then she "disappeared." I had not seen her for a few weeks. One Friday night I asked her sister to let her know that I would really like to meet her to have a conversation. She did come to see me the following Sunday, and we spoke.

A few days later, we spoke again. And she told me a very interesting story. She was so heartbroken and disappointed by the break-up, she had decided to commit suicide. The night she got the message that I wanted to talk to her was the night she had decided to end it all. She already had the weedicide at the side of her bed, intending to drink it later that night. As a courtesy to me, she decided to postpone drinking it so that she can respond to my request to meet with her.

Battered and Bruised but Still a Winner

Thankfully, after our conversation, she changed her mind.

Her decision to "end it all" is symptomatic of people who have seen their dreams collapse. They feel lost. They feel betrayed. They lose self-confidence. They are disillusioned by the thought of starting over. Sometimes they blame themselves. It is not as extreme as what Frankl describes in the concentration camps, but the emotional principles are the same: when a dearly-held dream falls apart, it leaves an indescribable hole in the heart. That hole in the heart creates different reactions from different people.

Some people experience the most devastating and traumatic experience and remain relatively calm, pull themselves together and resume the fight for their dreams. Other people seem to be dazed and completely shattered by a comparatively less severe and disappointing experience. This is what is described as emotional thresholds, different breaking points. People are different in countless ways. And one way is their emotional thresholds. Some have a higher tolerance for emotional let-downs than others. It is sometimes referred to a strength. I am a little cautious about using "strength" in that context because we may then be inclined to refer to someone with a lower emotional threshold as weak. It is not so simple. Different from does not necessarily mean weaker than.

What Shall We Become of Your Dreams

Those who are leaders, counselors, pastors, coaches, or in some way have the privilege of making an input in others' lives, must understand that not everybody handles pressure the same way. We can make the mistake of trivializing the reaction of those we are responsible for helping if we assess the reaction of one person by comparing it to another, based on similar circumstances. We all respond differently to the same emotional stimuli.

Regardless of where you are on the scale of emotional tolerance for challenges and failures, you need to be prepared for some roller-coaster moments on the road to your dream.

I remember another true story from my time as the youth leader. This couple appeared to be a perfect couple, as if out of a soap opera; a handsome young man and a very attractive young woman. She was well-educated and employed with a large financial company. They had two charming young boys.

One day, I was taken aback when I was approached to try to help them because they were having problems. They were not in my youth group but I was acquainted with both of them. They lived in a modern house with a beautiful yard and all modern facilities in the house. By the time I intervened, the husband had already moved out and living alone. I went to visit him and was shocked by what I saw. He was living in a shack without any modern facilities – minimal furniture, no electricity, and no running water. When I inquired about why he would leave a beautiful house to

Battered and Bruised but Still a Winner

live like that, his response was, "I am happier here."

Wounded people do strange things. In moments like these people need to know that they can bounce back; that God can use what looks like a major disappointment and direct them to a different, better future.

This type of brokenness is not only restricted to personal relationships. It could be the loss of a job, the failure of a business, major losses from an investment gone wrong, or any number of a life's experiences that are tragic or deeply hurtful.

A workplace is a place of dreams for most people. It is the environment where visions of great careers are born. It's the place that allows one to acquire a house, own a car, educate children and pay the bills. At the workplace, relationships are formed, contacts are established and a network of professional colleagues is developed. For most people, the job is at the center of their quality of life.

However, there are times when the job transforms from a place of dreams to a place of heartbreak. The competition for promotions, power, and perks makes some people descend to the darker side of humanity. Betrayal, back-stabbing, and discrimination can rob us of opportunities that we deserve. Unfairness and injustices may see us get sidelined, transferred, demoted, or even fired.

These moments are traumatic. But they are not beyond bouncing back. These are moments when we need to have confidence in ourselves, our skills, our integrity and, most importantly, our God. Keeping one's eye on one's dream and refocusing after a setback is key to the bounce back.

During His life and ministry, Jesus had to endure all manner of destructive attacks on His life and character. He was called the devil, a Sabbath-breaker, a false prophet, a hypocrite, they lied about Him and plotted to kill Him on numerous occasions.

The movie *The Passion of the Christ* gives a visual impression of how brutal the battering was before the actual crucifixion took place. And brutal it was. Isaiah describes it this way, "But many were amazed when they saw him. His face was so disfigured he seemed hardly human, and from his appearance, one would scarcely know he was a man."[34]

So why did He choose to go through that? A whole book could be written just in answer to that question. There could be deep theological and doctrinal expositions in answer to the question. But I want to emphasize just one from the book of Hebrews: "Let us keep our eyes on Jesus, the champion who initiates and perfects our faith. Because of the joy awaiting him, he endured the cross, disregarding its shame. Now he is seated in the place of honor beside God's throne."[35]

34 *Isaiah 52:14 NLT*
35 *Hebrews 12:2 NLT*

Battered and Bruised but Still a Winner

Observe "because of the joy awaiting him." He kept His focus on His mission, His purpose, His dream. And that pushed Him to endure extraordinary pain, shame, and suffering.

And He bounced back.

He won.

He is in a place of honor.

Be like Jesus.

Keep your eyes on the prize.

Chapter 10

ENCOURAGE YOURSELF

"Many of us have miscalculated the level of commitment our social circle had toward us, and we got left with our heads spinning. Like a bride, we sometimes get left at the altar. It's like getting stood-up on a date."

What Shall We Become of Your Dreams

"Yeah, this is the reason I almost gave up when I was betrayed. I can't understand what is lacking in me. I am educated. I am good inside and out. I am loyal and faithful, but it doesn't seem to be enough. Behind my smile, I have a sad life. That is the real inside of me. I have a lot of questions about my life. Why? You know it's hard to pretend and smile as if I'm okay, because I'm not okay."

That was the profound response to a simple, casual question via social media. The question was simply, "Why don't you smile in the pictures you post?" Because of my years of work with people who are pursuing their dreams, including those who are fighting to get back on track, I can detect hidden emotions behind certain facial expressions, body language, and certain words or phrases. You have heard of reading between the lines. Well, for me there are many more "in-betweens" to read: reading between the expressions, reading between the words, and reading between the social media posts.

Many people are longing to have someone who would care enough to ask, while others keep it all bottled up inside because they don't know who to trust. They have trusted in the past and were betrayed. There are some whose personalities, socialization, or upbringing taught them to "keep private matters private" so they choose not to talk it out with anyone. And there are those, among whom is a significant percentage of men, who think it is weakness or a blow to the ego to acknowledge a struggle, emotional pain, or a disappointing setback. But the weighty things that are bottled up inside often find expression in non-verbal clues and in the subtexts of social media posts. Many times the persons involved are not even conscious of the very effective ways they are unintentionally communicating.

So when I asked why there are no smiling photos on the page, I knew what to expect if that person was willing to be candid with me.

The response to my question underscored several things that we already established. Relationships are important. We all need people to love and people to love us. Friends, relatives, spouses, colleagues, mentors, neighbors, and pastors are some of the numerous people who make a contribution to our lives in some way. There is no denying that everybody needs somebody.

We have been socialized to be inspired by the words, actions, and achievements of others. We have pastors or other spiritual advisors. We have seniors on the job. We have mentors. We have life coaches and motivational speakers. We are inspired by people who have overcome tremendous odds and made it big. We have professionals that we depend on for input in specific areas of expertise such as doctors, lawyers, bankers, investment managers, etc.

Volumes of books have been written about motivation. In orga-

What Shall We Become of Your Dreams

nizations, leaders are trained to understand that a part of their responsibilities is to motivate others. Employees have also come to expect some type of tangible action; some type of intervention, strategy, or tactics by "the bosses" that are designed to motivate them. We have come to see motivation as an intervention by someone else to keep us enthused and engaged. Motivation is generally accepted as an external input into our lives. In the same way, a minister is expected to keep the flock inspired and fired up to maintain focus on their faith.

We are validated to a large extent by the views of others and our interactions with them.

All of that is correct and has a place in our lives. All adults, and many younger ones too, will face a personal crisis at some point in their lives; many will face multiple crises in the course of their lives. Intuitively, or by training, we acknowledge the possibility of future crises because a part of being a responsible person is to plan for the "rainy day." My father had two sons, and he always advised us to learn to cook and do household chores – to be self-sufficient – "because you never know what could happen."

Ready to Rumble

It is wonderful to have a shoulder to lean on. But there will come a time when none of the people that you have become accustomed to turning to are available or accessible. That's when your

Encourage Yourself

social circle is a flat line. Only you. There are likely to be moments when you stand alone, facing your crises, your struggles, and the pursuit of your dreams – or your broken dreams – all by your lonesome. Then what do you do?

Be a boxer. A boxer has a trainer, a coach, a dietitian, a doctor, an attorney, an agent, a manager, a publicist, and many more handlers. The boxer may have millions of adoring fans around the world and thousands in the stadium cheering him on. He has trusted professionals in his corner outside the ring. There may be people lining up for autographs or selfies with him. He may be a little child's hero, the person someone is referring to when she says, "I want to be like that when I grow up."

But when the boxer gets in the ring to fight, he or she fights alone. In the ring, you can draw upon all the inputs from a lot of people, draw upon past experiences and your personal skills. But you are fighting alone. All the decisions you make in the ring, you make alone. You decide when to duck, when to move away, when to punch, when to skip or when to jump. You have to decide all by yourself what punches to throw and when. Is it going to be a jab, an uppercut, a cross, or a hook? You have to motivate yourself. You have to encourage yourself. And you have to fight for your life, your career, your reputation, and your paycheck, all by yourself.

Winning or losing is up to you when you are in the ring. By

What Shall We Become of Your Dreams

yourself. There's no partner to tag who will jump in and help you when it looks like you are going down. That's somebody else's fight. Your fight is alone.

There will be times when you call the person who you depend on the most and all you get is an automated voice, "The number you have reached does not answer." There will be times when your bestie is otherwise engaged and cannot accommodate you. There will be times when your pastor is unreachable. In these times, you have to go it alone.

In 1 Samuel Chapter 30, we find encouragement for standing alone.

> David and his men came to the city and it was burned by fire. Their wives and their sons and their daughters were captured and taken away. Then David and the people that were with him lifted up their voices and wept until they had no more power to weep. And David was greatly distressed because the people spoke of stoning him because all the people were in grief. But David encouraged himself in the Lord his God.[36]

David was in a moment of great distress with no one to help him. On the contrary, those around him turned on him. He had to become a boxer – in the ring fighting by himself. He had to motivate himself, support himself, and counsel himself: "but David

36 *1 Samuel 30:3-6*

encouraged himself…" There will be times when the only person you can count on is you. There will be times when those who you thought were on your team, turn on you. There will be times when you will say, "I never expected that from them."

It's Complicated

There are countless stories of people whose support system, or the support system they thought they had, disappeared – they get ghosted. Then they are left facing daunting challenges without the help on which they relied when they took on the challenge. Many of us have miscalculated the level of commitment our social circle had toward us, and we got left with our heads spinning. Like a bride, we sometimes get left at the altar. It's like getting stood-up on a date. In moments like these, you have to draw on your personal strength, have confidence in your God, and fight like a warrior to survive, fight like a warrior for your dream, fight for your life.

When Jesus was in active ministry it was difficult for Him to get some time alone. He was always surrounded by crowds and meeting all manner of the people's needs. To get some time alone, He had to get up before sunrise and go into a secluded place. His disciples promised Him that they would never leave His side, even if it cost them their lives. But when He was arrested, this was their reaction, "At that point, all the disciples

What Shall We Become of Your Dreams

deserted him and fled."[37] Jesus ended up facing the darkest, most painful moment of His life without any of His supporters within sight. He fought His biggest battle alone.

When people in your circle abandon you or do not rise to the level that you expected, do not interpret it as a reflection on the potential of your dream or your personal worth. People react to you and issues related to you based on their own self-interests, their own fears and limitations. Do not let other people's inability to maintain the commitments they have made to you as friends diminish the value of your dream or reduce your enthusiasm. You do you, and let them do them.

Do not give too much power to other people over your emotions, otherwise you become captive to their whims. Sure, it would be so much better if we have solid friends (or relatives, or spouses, or colleagues, or employers) who stick with us through the moments when we are most vulnerable, but if it does not work out that way, and sometimes it doesn't, do not let it cause you to slow your walk. Keep moving.

Like David, you might be weeping. But you still have to fight. Broken, but still have to fight. Stabbed in the back, but still have to fight. Bleeding inside, but still have to fight. Because you have a dream to fight for, and you are not giving up. You either fight or lose. And you are not a loser.

---

37 Matthew 26:56 NLT

Encourage Yourself

Let's reflect again on the experience David had that I quoted previously: "Then David and the people that were with him lifted up their voices and wept until they had no more power to weep."[38] David was hurt, in pain, and weeping "until he had no more power to weep," just like the others who were with him. But that did not prevent them from turning on him; "...the people spoke of stoning him..."

Sometimes the people around us are so engrossed in their own pain that they don't see the pain of others. This is especially so when you are the leader. Pain often makes people look for someone or something to blame, and sometimes the blame is misdirected, and the leader is often the target of choice. Innocent people could get caught in the crossfire. It's a sort of catharsis that takes place: an emotional release, releasing or expressing strong emotions.

I remember the time when I was "the boss" and a location for which I was responsible experienced an armed robbery. The robbers not only took the company's cash, but also the personal property of the staff. As is expected of senior managers, I visited the location to lend some support. During the staff meeting, one staff member lashed out. He raised his voice, shouting at me and criticizing me personally, as well as the company in general. In a loud voice, he raised all sorts of issues that in his opinion showed that we didn't care. He blamed me and the company for the robbery.

---

38 1Samuel 30:4 KJV

His behaviour would normally be considered offensive and disrespectful. But I understood the moment. After the emotions subsided, I explained to him that he was lashing out at the wrong people. The people responsible for his trauma and his loss were the robbers. We were on the same side. I was his friend. We were all victims. The company suffered losses too. If we turned on each other, we lost sight of the real culprits, the bandits.

Pain often makes people look for someone or something to blame, and the leader is often the target of choice.

Some of the staff were concerned that I would chastise the person who lost his cool. I told them that we need to understand the state of mind: "I have never had a gun pointed at my face. I have never been in the situation where I felt that in a split second I could get my brains blown out, so let us move on." His shouting at me was a form of catharsis for him.

Celebrate Yourself

There are many stories of people who have given their all to their job; they have served the company well. Much of their skills and experience were developed with that company. They have friends there. They have built their lives around the job – home, school, and social life. And then they get fired or laid off.

If that is you, you feel lost. "How do I start over after all these

Encourage Yourself

years? I don't even know where to start to look. I have a family. I have bills." Many of your outreaches to other employers turn up empty. But you know what? It's your life, it's your dream, and you will fight. Because it's either you fight or you lose.

We often see this in families. Years were invested in a relationship and then out of the blue, things fall apart. For many, losing the relationship is one thing, but losing everything else is another thing. Many are left to start over virtually penniless. Often one party finds himself or herself scrambling to find a home and struggling to cope with new routines and still focus on the things that are important to them.

Many are the stories about "nasty divorces." Both parties go after each, trying to extract everything that they can from each other. It is bewildering trying to understand how a couple goes from honeymoon to hell; from starry-eyed love, romance, and intimacy to bitter feuding, doing everything to destroy the other person. In the end, both are damaged, and often broken and lonely.

You find yourself looking at dating sites. But you are concerned about being recognized by friends or colleagues. This is very complicated. It's a double whammy. "Where do I find another relationship at my age; after all these years? How do I recover my finances? How do I pay my bills? How do I support myself? I cannot steal and I am too proud to beg." But you hold your chin up, you pull yourself together, and you fight. Alone.

What Shall We Become of Your Dreams

Fighting alone could be the toughest thing you will ever do in your life. But when you win, there is a measure of satisfaction and self-confidence that is incomparable. You feel like you can go on the top of a mountain and shout to the world. You feel like you have a story to tell. You want to testify. You want to write a book. You wish you can create a viral social media post to celebrate the new you. You want to reach out to others in a similar predicament and say, "Fight brother, fight. There's a big world of opportunity out there. Go for it." Or the ladies might say, "You go girl! Don't let anyone dim your light."

It is in the lonely moments, if you choose not to reveal your pain to others or if no one is there for you, you have to encourage yourself. If we have a choice, we should always seek help. But there are times we don't have a choice, when there is no one to turn to, so we fight alone. Don't be afraid to fight alone if you have to. Be your best supporter. Applaud yourself. And soon, when you succeed, an audience will be giving the applause.

One source of major disappointment is when we look for support from the people who we have helped along the way. I have heard statements similar to this a lot of times, "After all the things I did for him, I expected some support."

If you are expecting the same people you help to always be there to help you, you might be sorely disappointed. It doesn't always work that way. The people who you help are like seeds

Encourage Yourself

you sow. It will come back to you but not necessarily from the same source. Jesus said in the Book of Luke, "Give, and it shall be given unto you; good measure, pressed down, shaken together, and running over, shall men give into your bosom."[39] It says, "shall men give into your bosom," not the same men shall give.

Some years ago, a young man came to the church where I was attending at the time, and I developed an acquaintance with him. I visited his home one day and was appalled at the living conditions in his house. Actually, it wasn't much of a house. The walls were made of dirt, the floor was made of dirt, there was no real furniture or kitchen appliances. He wanted to get married but that house was in no state to accommodate his bride.

After some discussions with him, I decided to help him. Because I had a good credit rating and he had none, I took him to a hire purchase store and signed as a guarantor for him to outfit an apartment and get married. He got a bed, a stove, a dining table, and a refrigerator. Then he got married and moved in. He was supposed to pay the monthly installments for the items.

Sometime later, something upset him at the church, and he became angry and bitter. He took his precious time to go to the homes of several members of the church and tried to get them to stop attending. He was particularly critical of me and my relatives. Then one day while I was at home, an officer of the court came to my house to serve me a writ. I was sued by the store be-

39 *Luke 6:38 KJV*

What Shall We Become of Your Dreams

cause the gentleman had stopped making the monthly payments. Because I was the guarantor, I had to dip into my savings and pay for all the items in his apartment.

Imagine the scenario: after he had spent hours going from one home to the other saying bad things about me, he would go home and get a refreshing drink from a refrigerator that I paid for and go to sleep on a bed that I paid for.

But that did not stop me from helping other people who were within my ability to help, although my experience with my friend was a head-scratcher. For a moment, one might wonder, "Is it worth it? I try to help, I get the messy end of the stick by having to pay all those bills, and then have my character under attack by the person I tried to help." There may be some moments of contemplation and sleepless nights. And when the next opportunity arises to help someone, you may hesitate, "Ummm, ah, I'm not sure. Let me think about it. I'll get back to you."

On reflection you are likely to conclude that you should not refuse to help one person because of another person's ingratitude. Then you do whatever you can, in the full knowledge that the blessings from helping someone do not necessarily return from the source to which you gave. It hardly ever works out that way.

The people you help may not be there to help you in time of need but Matthew assures us that God has it registered: "And if you give even a cup of cold water to one of the least of my follow-

Encourage Yourself

ers, you will surely be rewarded."[40] So keep your focus on your dream because help will come, even from unexpected sources.

Life is great when there's a shoulder to lean on.

But sometimes there's no shoulder.

Be like a boxer.

Fight alone.

And win.

---

40 *Matthew 10:42 NLT*

Chapter 11

I FEEL INVISIBLE

"Someone can have a lengthy in-person conversation with you and not realize that you fell asleep crying the night before. Others may never know that behind that beautiful smile is someone who is going home to cry."

I Feel Invisible

Based on anecdotal evidence, my conclusion is that there is likely to be many more emotionally hurting people than there are physically sick people among the people with whom we routinely interact. You see, physical wounds are often easily identifiable. It is easy to recognize that a hand is broken, a neck is in a brace, or someone is using a wheelchair. People also tend to be more open with their physical ailments. We make deliberate efforts to assist those who are physically hurt. It is just the courteous thing to do.

But it's a different kettle of fish with people who are hurting emotionally.

If you are in a group and one person in the group gets hurt and starts to bleed, everyone stops and rushes to render aid. If it's a party, the party is over, if not for everybody, at least for some who will rush to help. If someone is at a podium making a speech, the speech is paused once the speaker is aware that someone in the audience is hurt and bleeding. Because they see blood. If you are talking to someone and suddenly blood starts to ooze from that person's nose, you are likely to spring into action, "Oh my God! You are bleeding! Here's a rag. Let's call a doctor. Let's call an ambulance." You spring into action because you see blood. Physical wounds or visible signs of hurt or injury attract help. Fast.

What Shall We Become of Your Dreams

Special attention for people with physical disabilities is woven into our civility and the laws in most developed and developing countries of the world. They have reserved parking. Public buildings must be designed to accommodate them and a whole lot of other unique provisions are made for them. All of this is correct and noble.

But there is no special treatment for people who are hurting inside unless that hurt is visibly manifested. You don't see a parking space reserved for people who are brokenhearted and discouraged. Someone can have a lengthy in-person conversation with you and not realize that you fell asleep crying the night before. Others may never know that behind that beautiful smile is someone who is going home to cry. Someone can be seated next to you in the church and not realize that you are struggling to hold your life together. Such a person may be in the cubicle next to yours at the office.

If there is an auto accident in the street, passersby will slow down and look. If they don't see injuries, they just keep driving. But if they see injuries and blood, they are likely to stop to help. On the other hand, we can pass scores, or even hundreds, of hurting people on a busy street and we pay absolutely no attention to them because we don't see blood. Their wounds are invisible.

It is a crime to physically hurt someone. There's a wide range of criminal descriptions for those who physically hurt others.

I Feel Invisible

You can be convicted and end up in jail for just touching someone. On the job, you are likely to be immediately fired if you knock down a colleague with your fist. But it's not a crime to hurt someone emotionally. How many people have been fired for playing politics and causing severe emotional pain to others? How many managers have been fired for playing favorites and by-passing more deserving candidates for promotion, even though this causes significant emotional wounds to those who are unfairly treated? Very rare, if at all. However, if that same manager physically attacks his employee, he will be fired.

It's hard to get action from Human Resources when you are humiliated, insulted, or disrespected because the wounds caused by these behaviors are not visible and the "burden of proof" is extremely high. You are likely to be told to toughen up and get over it.

When you are hurting emotionally, unless you break down and cry, you can be invisible; numerous people can pass by without seeing you. Help is not readily available or easily offered.

It is similar when you are dreaming. It is difficult for others to see your dream because your dream is in your heart. You may be ignored, by-passed, mocked or become the subject of derision. In the eyes of others, you may not look like the type of person who can make it big. When they are looking for high-potential persons, you are not the one that makes it to the shortlist. You seem to be always the bridesmaid and never the bride; always the Cinderella who is kept out of the limelight.

You are invisible twice. Once because many don't see the potential of your dreams, and secondly, because nobody sees the pain of being bypassed or overlooked.

Invisible at Work

I always had big dreams for myself. In my career, I aimed for excellence to the best of my ability. I was disciplined as far as attendance and punctuality go. I was rarely late and seldom absent. I think I produced good quality and quantity of work. In addition, I was virtually always studying and improving my academic qualifications in areas that were directly relevant to my job.

At one time, I was the second most senior person in my division of the business when a senior level position opened up. I do not subscribe to the notion that attributes like seniority, age, or tenure automatically qualifies someone for promotion. I think that the more relevant criteria are things like track record, proven competence, ethical conduct, team orientation, and integrity. I thought that I had all those attributes.

The job was somewhat of a once-in-a-long-time opportunity. It

I Feel Invisible

would put the successful person in an ideal place for future upward mobility, in addition to the significant salary and perks. I thought I was a shoo-in for the position. My colleagues thought so as well. So I was all smiles every day, waiting to be called and given the great news. Then I realized that I was invisible! While I was seeing my dream job very clearly within reach, another person or other people were not seeing me at all. I was bypassed and someone from outside the organization was hired to fill the vacancy. She had little familiarity with what we did in that division. She took up the job and got a nice office while I remained in my cubicle, still the go-to person in the division because of my knowledge and track record.

Well, that was a disappointing and unpleasant experience, a real bummer as some might say. Somebody burst my bubble, big time. I was very disappointed. I couldn't rationalize what went into the decision-making. As is somewhat normal in these cases, there was speculation about office politics and nepotism. These things do have a powerful impact on how things are done in organizations, but that is not always the case. Sometimes people genuinely have different perspectives of the same scenario. Whether it was office politics or not, it was a definite blow to my career dreams.

However, from my early teenage days, when I started to take my faith seriously and pray in the name of Jesus, I developed a reli-

What Shall We Become of Your Dreams

ance on God to take me through tough times. So I found solace in my prayers and continued to dream. I tried not to develop any negative chip-on-the-shoulder attitudes and continued to do my job to the best of my ability.

Then in just three months, the lady suddenly quit. I will never know, but I think she saw the critical role that I played in the division and she had the opportunity to assess my competence and concluded that something was odd about her appointment. If that was indeed so, quitting was an extremely noble thing for her to do. But for me, my smile returned. I was now walking around, saying quietly in my mind, "Let me see how they are going to bypass me this time. I am no longer invisible. I am as visible as the morning sun." (This is where we would put "Lol" or a laughing emoji if this was a social media post.)

As they say, to cut a long story short, the wheels of the organization turned, and I got the promotion –and the office, and the salary, and the perks. It was an answer to prayer and another example of God looking after His own. That appointment set in motion a sequence of events that helped my career take off, with several quicker-than-usual promotions to very senior levels of the company. I was living my career dreams.

There will be times when the world doesn't see you, when you are dreaming dreams that only you can see. There will be times when the confidence that you have in yourself doesn't match what your environment tells you that you should have. It would appear as if the universe doubts you and that unseen forces are arrayed against you, pushing you down a path that is contrary to where you want to go.

There are times you would wonder if even God is not supporting your dream. You will silently say to yourself, "If God is in this, why didn't it work out? Maybe God wants something different for me." And maybe He does. But if He does, He will use the moments that look like failures, the path that looks like a dead-end, and direct your circumstances so that you still end up in the place of your dreams.

One of the toughest battles you will ever face in your life is the feeling that your dream is collapsing around you and that nobody is on your side. But one of the most powerful persons in the world is the person who is so convinced that a dream is realizable, that he or she is willing to challenge the world. This is one of life's great defining moments that all of us will face in some form.

How I Learned to See Invisible People

Tillo was a recovering former drug-dependent person who lived not far from my office. He would hang around the office and in the nearby streets, just passing the time. His drug problem had

What Shall We Become of Your Dreams

somewhat marginalized him, and therefore he had no job. Despite his challenges, he had a calm personality, was well-mannered and didn't pose a threat to anyone. By hanging around the office complex, some of the staff got to know him and trust him somewhat.

Then he asked me to allow him to wash the managers' cars that were usually parked in the basement. At that time, we needed someone to wash the cars twice a week and I allowed him to wash mine, and with the agreement of the other managers, he also started washing theirs. Some non-managerial staff also chose to let him wash their cars. This became his regular job during the week.

This day it was Christmas Eve and, as usual, he was in the basement washing the cars. We were in the office experiencing Christmas cheer and exchanging gifts with laughter, hugs, good wishes, food, and drinks. It was the usual feeling of warmth and love that pervades the atmosphere at Christmastime. Then for some reason which I cannot now recall, I went to the basement to obtain something from my car. I saw Tillo washing the cars, and I greeted him as I would usually do. Then something happened that has had a lasting impact on me.

Tillo burst into tears. He was crying and talking in a somewhat loud voice (I am paraphrasing his dialect), "Mr. Cuffie, you all don't understand! Look at me, everybody is having fun. Everybody is enjoying themselves and I am just here. I have nobody,

I Feel Invisible

I have nothing."

I was a very revealing moment. I left the basement, walked to a nearby supermarket, purchased a variety of items that are popular at Christmastime, got assistance from the staff at the office, and hurriedly prepared a gift hamper for him.

But the hamper is not the point. The point is Tillo and his loneliness, his emptiness, and the lack of family in his life were invisible to me, even at the very sentimental time that was Christmas. If I had discerned his state of mind before and proactively bought him a gift and made him feel special, the tears may not have flowed. I was aware of his background, the challenges he was facing to rebuild his life, but I still didn't see beyond the "car wash guy." How many hurting people are in our circle every day and we are not seeing them? We may be aware of their presence but not actually seeing them and not seeing beneath the surface. There may be people around us who are crying, just not audibly, and we are neither hearing nor seeing them.

How do we see the cries for help without being nosy or without overly prying? Let us pray that God helps us see the invisible people in our circle. For some people, their dream is simply to be appreciated; to be seen.

What Shall We Become of Your Dreams

Another life-changing experience happened around the same time. Dave was a clerical person at the office who also had some responsibilities that required him to drive a company car. He was one of the most cheerful and funny guys at the office. He was involved in all our department's extra-curricular sporting or social activities. We used to have a fun tell-a-joke competition for Father's Day every year, and since he came to the department, he was always a participant in the joke competition.

One Friday, my car was being repaired and I asked him to give me a ride to a meeting at our head office a few miles away. That day, Dave was unusually quiet. He was not his usual cheerful self. I observed his demeanor but I said nothing. I thought that he was just "not himself" on that day. Then, on the Saturday night, I got a call from his supervisor. Dave had committed suicide.

What if I had reached out to him and inquired what was the matter? If he was given the chance to talk about it, would it have been any different? I will never know. But this experience made me much more conscious of the need to look beneath the surface whenever there is a moment like that. Tillo and Dave helped shaped how I see others in my circle. I am now more aware of the invisible people around me.

I Feel Invisible

There are things that we can't see with our eyes.

There are things that are seen with the heart.

A sensitive heart.

Otherwise, people around us are invisible.

Take a look around.

Chapter 12

MAJORING IN MINORS

"There are countless Christians who have killed their ministries, forfeited their callings, buried their gifts, and destroyed strong friendships because they didn't have the emotional stability or spiritual maturity to weather the storm of a temporary season of disenchantment."

Majoring in Minors

When I was a little kid, we used to say this nursery rhyme in school.

Pussy cat, pussy cat, where have you been?
I've been to London to visit the Queen.
Pussy cat, pussy cat, what did you there?
I frightened a little mouse under her chair.

The poem is thought to have been first published way back in 1805. There are various stories about what inspired it and what is its true meaning, but it has survived through generations as a kids' favorite.

Now as an adult, when I reflect on this nursery rhyme, I see a powerful lesson with real-world parallels. The cat goes to visit the queen. The queen lives in Buckingham Palace. This is an iconic building with a long marvelous history. Decisions and activities at Buckingham Palace have affected the history and direction of the world.

There are impeccably manicured grounds, unique historic architectural designs, the majestic throne room, the grand staircase, and the beautiful chandeliers. Then there are the Royal Guards with their distinctive red tunic and bearskin headgear, and the royal family themselves.

There is a lot to see and explore at Buckingham Palace. But the cat can only identify one of the tiniest, most inconspicuous things to give its attention and single out for mention – a mouse under the chair. It is because of the nature of the cat. That is its level of interest, and that is what it is naturally drawn toward.

That reminds me of one of the reasons that many dreams are lost, many relationships suffer, many careers are ruined and many churches experience divisions and splits: the tendency of some among us to focus on insignificant trivialities, as if it is their nature to ignore the numerous wonderful things around them and focus on the minor ones. As we often say, they major in the minors.

These are people who display an unpredictable emotional state which often manifests itself in being easily offended and focusing on the minor things. Being emotionally stable is an extremely desirable trait if one is to maintain the type of laser-like focus on one's goals and dreams. Emotional stability refers to the ability to remain calm, controlled and balanced when facing disruptive circumstances in the pursuit of one's objectives. On the contrary, emotional instability makes one prone to sudden mood swings; one can move from calm, to agitated, to angry in a short time with only minor stimuli.

There are some homes where an emotionally unpredictable person makes the home a very tense place. The home is your safe place; the place where you should be able to find peace and relaxation, where you can unclutter the mind from all the issues

Majoring in Minors

and challenges that come from a routine day of work, school, or business. It should be the place where you laugh, be your silly self, and experience warmth and love. But often there's that one person in the home who, when he or she enters, an atmosphere of tension takes over; everybody gets quiet, the laughter ceases, and they are walking on eggshells, afraid that that person might explode over something small. That person may need help.

It is similar at the workplace. Most business leaders would have experienced having that one person who is frequently upset about something trivial, the constant complainer; the one who causes you to keep your fingers crossed at staff meetings, who seems impossible to please. The one who, when absent, the office feels like a happy family.

Such is the power of emotional instability.

In my experience, a lot of dreams are obstructed, stalled, or dead because the dreamer displays an emotionally unstable temperament. Once I was told that a good friend of mine, who was a very talented musician and singer, left his church. I went to talk to him to find out what was the problem. He told me that he didn't like how the pastor looked at him and that he found that the pastor was "moving strange." This was an extremely subjective and trivial reason but he walked away from serving, disrupted a local church, and caused emotional distress.

What Shall We Become of Your Dreams

I have first-hand knowledge of numerous instances where people have sabotaged their dreams and those of others by being offended by minor issues. These types of trivialities have been known to explode into bigger conflicts, leaving a trail of wounded hearts and lost dreams.

Christian believers who claim to be advocates for love, healing, and forgiveness have often fallen victims to the exact opposite values. They sing defiant songs about trampling the devil and casting out demons but then undermine their dreams by being offended by small misunderstandings. It will do us well to remember the question Jeremiah asked, "If racing against mere men makes you tired, how will you race against horses? If you stumble and fall on open ground, what will you do in the rough terrain?"[41]

Then there are those who are so thin-skinned that they get offended by the most routine correction. They forget the sharp rebuke Jesus once gave to Peter. As told by Matthew, Jesus looked Peter in the eye and said, "Get away from me, Satan! You are a dangerous trap to me. You are seeing things merely from a human point of view, not from God's."[42] Imagine a pastor being that direct today!

And what about this from the book of wisdom, Proverbs: "Correct the wise, and they will love you; instruct the wise and they

---

41 Jeremiah 12:5 NLT
42 Matthew 16:23 NLT

Majoring in Minors

will be even wiser."[43]

Blowing-Up a Promising Career

Ricky was a young university graduate. He was well-dressed and articulate during the interview at the company where I worked. He was easily the best candidate that I interviewed, and he was hired. It proved to be a good choice. He brought excellent attributes to the job; creativity, initiative, and new ideas.

It wasn't very long before a position opened, and he was promoted. He was ecstatic. It was the achievement of a career dream. The new job had very important deliverables, it was in a growing division because its mandate represented the future of the company, but with it came a certain amount of pressure to meet deadlines. He was well placed for upward mobility.

Then he started to unravel. The pressure was getting to him. He would get testy when corrected. He would pout when pushed for urgent deliverables. Then he started to absent himself from work in apparent protest when things didn't go his way. His emotional instability was eroding his reputation. It was depreciating his value as an employee. Attempts to give him advice and guidance were rebuffed. After a period of time, his emotional responses to the demands of the job became unsustainable, and he had to go. He lost sight of a promising career and the big opportunities

---

43 Proverbs 9:8-9 NLT

What Shall We Become of Your Dreams

that were ahead of him and instead got distracted by the "mouse under the chair," the routine minor pressures that are part of professional life.

Most leaders have had to deal with a Ricky. Whether in church, a charity, a sports team, or any team-based organization, most leaders can identify people like Ricky, regardless of gender, who failed to maximize their potential because of their propensity to be thin-skinned. They gripe, they are frequent complainers, they see all the negatives, they are argumentative, they irritate everybody. The inability to control one's emotions can be detrimental to one's dream. It may even be something that requires much prayer and/or professional help to mitigate or prevent the unpleasant consequences that will inevitably arise.

All of us need to develop emotional resilience if we are to achieve our goals. Emotional resilience is the ability to sustain stressful situations and tough experiences and still remain focused on one's goals. Emotionally resilient people are able to cope with uncertainty or demanding situations with calm and aplomb. That's possibly why God told Joshua that he had be strong and very courageous if he wanted to be successful. Dreams require strength.

One cannot be an effective leader if one is emotionally unstable. Leaders face all sorts of pressures, are under a lot of scrutiny, and have to make countless decisions of varying impact. There-

Majoring in Minors

fore, developing a balanced temperament is critical if one wants to ascend to, or remain in, positions of leadership in any sphere – community, politics, business, or ecclesiastical.

Some of the most famous and admired people in the world were emotionally stable and emotionally resilient people. Think Martin Luther King Jr. Think Mahatma Gandhi. Think Nelson Mandela. Even though Nelson Mandela was considered by his detractors to be a terrorist of sorts when he was arrested, on his release from prison after twenty-seven years, he is quoted as saying, "When I walked out the gates of the prison that day, if I harbored hate and bitterness in my heart, I would still be in prison." Incredible emotional control.

This Dream Will Self-Destruct in 5 Seconds...

In the book of Second Samuel,[44] we meet Ahithophel, who we shall call Arthy only because "Ahithophel" is difficult to pronounce. Arthy was an advisor to kings. He was once a trusted advisor to King David but later defected to Absalom. Arthy was well known and very respected for his wisdom, foresight, and discernment. So impressive was his keen sense of perception, this is how he is described in Chapter 16: "Absalom followed Arthy's advice just as David had done. For every word Arthy spoke seemed as wise as though it had come directly from the

---

44 2 Samuel 17 & 18

mouth of God." Arthy was indeed a man who was in a class all by himself.

Absalom was David's son, but unfortunately, even as it is today, there are sometimes bitter conflicts and rivalry between family members. He was at war with David, and he was consulting with Arthy in devising strategies and tactics for a battle plan. Arthy outlined his plan: "With a contingent of 12,000 men, I will go after David tonight. I am confident his men will panic and flee. And when they do, I will kill David. Then there will be peace." Absalom and all the elders of Israel liked Arthy's plan.

But before proceeding with Arthy's plan, Absalom requested a second opinion. He asked to bring in a guy by the name of Hushai. Absalom asked Hushai, "What do you think? Should we follow Arthy's plan? If not, what do you suggest?"

"Well," Hushai replied to Absalom, "this time Arthy has made a mistake. You know your father and his men; they are mighty warriors. Right now they are as enraged as a mother bear who has been robbed of her cubs. And remember that your father is an experienced man of war.

"I recommend that you mobilize the entire army of Israel. That way you will have an army as numerous as the sand on the seashore. And I advise that you personally lead the troops."

So Absalom and the men of Israel were persuaded and concluded that Hushai's plan was better than Arthy's.

When Arthy heard that his advice was rejected in favor of Hushai's, he felt humiliated. He was the preferred source of advice for years. He was revered by kings and commoners. His ego was deeply wounded by the rejection of his plan. And this was the result, "When Arthy realized that his advice had not been followed, he saddled his donkey, went to his hometown, set his affairs in order, and hanged himself. He died there and was buried in the family tomb."

This is my point. Arthy lacked emotional resilience. His ego got the better of him. He was not tough enough to survive rejection and bounce back. Instead, he killed himself, and all his dreams.

We can't bounce back if we are dead. We need to understand that there will be moments of great disappointment in our lives and when they happen, instead of killing our dreams, we must move to the next phase, plotting a bounce-back. Even in defeat, we must be planning for future victories.

There are countless Christians who have killed their ministries, forfeited their callings, buried their gifts, and destroyed strong friendships because they didn't have the emotional stability or spiritual maturity to weather the storm of a temporary season of disenchantment.

There are careers that have been ruined because of an overreac-

What Shall We Become of Your Dreams

tion to a temporary period of difficulty. There are many families that have been permanently torn apart, with relatives at war with each other, because of the inability of one or more of them to remain calm in periods of conflict.

We may never know how many marriages have ended in divorce because of emotional instability; the inability to work through short-term difficult situations. From my experience, there are couples who have had long and bitter divorces and when all is said and done, they still love each other. Because they overreacted to some of the pressures of marriage and gave too much attention to little things – the "mouse under the chair."

Be very cautious with taking decisions that affect you permanently based on temporary conditions. Don't misunderstand a short-term season to be a long-term experience, otherwise you are likely to make the wrong decision in managing the short-term. Don't self-destruct. Because if you self-destruct, so does your dream. Forever.

Now the stunning conclusion to the story of Arthy, Absalom, and Hushai. In a moment of despair when his plan was rejected by Absalom and others, Arthy hanged himself. He took a permanent, irreversible decision based on a single moment of despondency. But Arthy's plan was indeed the better plan! God was not in support of Absalom, and He allowed Absalom to adopt Hushai's plan, which was the wrong plan, so that he (Absalom)

Majoring in Minors

would be defeated.

This is what 2 Samuel 17:14 (NLT) says, "For the Lord had determined to defeat the counsel of Arthy, *which really was the better plan*, so that He could bring disaster on Absalom!" This means that the Lord caused Absalom to reject Arthy's plan, *even though Arthy's plan was the better military plan*, because the Lord wanted Absalom to be defeated. The rejection of Arthy's plan by Absalom was not a rejection of Arthy or the wisdom of his plan, rather it was the work of God. It did not mean that Arthy had lost his wisdom and strategic war-fighting skills. His plan was actually the better plan. There was a bigger spiritual plan that God was working out. But Arthy took the rejection of his plan too personally.

If Arthy had controlled his ego, if he had been a little emotionally tougher, if he had been a little more patient, he would have lived to be vindicated. He would have come to realize that his plan was better all along.

Don't be Arthy.

Have patience and be strong in the tough times. Sometimes for a moment in time, we don't know what God is up to, but He is always working on our behalf.

It's safe to say that most people in the world have heard of Judas. After betraying Jesus, he realized that he made a mistake. And

What Shall We Become of Your Dreams

in terms of the approach when one makes a mistake, Judas did all the right things: he repented, he was remorseful, he returned the money that he was paid, he confessed he was wrong; "I have sinned because I have betrayed an innocent man."[45] Yet he went out and hanged himself.

Don't be Judas.

Peter also let down Jesus, although his actions were not as extreme as Judas' betrayal. After promising vehemently that he would stand by Jesus and never leave His side, he did exactly the opposite, and more loudly and more vehemently than his promise! He lied, and cursed, and angrily disowned Jesus. Three times. It was quite a scene. Then when reality hit him, he was distraught. His failure pierced his conscience, and he wept bitterly. But he did not hang himself.

Somehow, he endured his frustration and waited on an opportune moment to bounce back. And he bounced back in spectacular fashion. So dominant was he in the early church that he is considered by some Christians to be the first Pope.

Be like Peter.

When we disappoint ourselves, we can get totally dejected. Our feelings of regret can impede our cognitive abilities, obscure our vision and we often cannot see a way out. This could drive us to

---

45 Matthew 27:4 NLT

Majoring in Minors

abandon our dreams and walk away. We are at a fork in the road: on the left is Judas and on the right is Peter. Choose to take Peter's road. Bide your time and look to the future when you will rise again and exceed all expectations. Don't kill your dream.

We are emotional beings.

We get hurt. We get disappointed.

But we have dreams.

We have to be strong. We have to bounce back.

The dead cannot dream.

To live is to dream.

Live your life.

Chapter 13

PLEASE DON'T JUDGE ME

"I don't think that most people enter marriage intending to get a divorce. Most people sincerely believe in 'till death do us part.' But unfortunately, things sometimes fall apart despite the best intentions at the start."

Please Don't Judge Me

Have you ever built a house? Many of us have. And if you haven't, you have probably seen one being built. There is a blueprint of the house that is guiding the builder. But to those who are unfamiliar with reading blueprints, it may just look like a lot of lines with a sprinkling of technical terms. But the architect, the builder, and the owner have a clear picture in their minds. They know exactly where it is going to end.

During early construction, the site is a mess: heavy equipment, dirt, dust, mud, debris, noise, nothing that resembles the impeccable picture of a lovely home with a loving family. But it would be a mistake to judge the vision at the foundation stage. One has to wait a while, endure the unsightliness and the apparent chaos before the final dream house emerges.

One of the challenges of building your dream is that you will be judged by those who don't know what the final version of your dream looks like. At some stage of your life, it might look all messed-up and confusing, even chaotic, but you know where you are going. The dreamer must also understand that the messiness of the foundation is not a reflection of the final destination.

One of the unfortunate tendencies of human nature is the propensity to judge others without understanding their story, or before a complete picture emerges. Stories that are imaginary and ill-informed are created and whispered in the community, the office grapevine, and even the church. When these stories get

What Shall We Become of Your Dreams

back to you, they can be distressing. But you know your dream so you keep going. And since you are emotionally stable, you smile to yourself and say, "Just wait 'till I'm done, and we'll see who has the last laugh."

I remember my parents, particularly my father, when we were growing up. He was a man of very humble means. He always had simple jobs. He could not afford any of the finer things in life. He literally wore rags because he prioritized taking care of his six children over himself. His prized possession was an old bicycle that was his way of getting around, riding miles upon miles every day. The house in which we grew up was just four walls of raw bricks with no furniture inside.

And he was judged for his poverty. He was mocked sometimes, laughed at sometimes, and treated unfairly sometimes. But you see, he had a dream for his children. His dream was simply that his children would have a better life than he did. While he couldn't build a great physical house, he was building the "house" of his family. But many were distracted by the chaos of the foundation and couldn't see his dream. So he made sure we went to school, even with the most meager amount of books, clothes, shoes, and even meals. Eventually his "house" was completed, and this is an overview of the "building":

While he was literate, he never had any certification, but most of his children and grandchildren have post-graduate qualifications.

While he only had a permanent job for about five years of his long life, his children have reached the highest levels of their careers from an early age.

While he never owned property, most of his children have acquired their own homes.

When you are being judged by persons who don't understand the stage of your dream, just keep calm and carry on. Your appearance may be judged by those who don't know that you spent a sleepless night with a sick child. You may not wear the most elegant clothes because you are managing a tight budget and focusing on the priorities of your dream at a particular point.

You have your personal definition of self-care, and though it may not meet the standard of the mean people who enjoy judging others, you are seeing the future state of yourself, your family, your ministry, or your business. So you are staying the course, writing your story, and shutting out judgmental people, even though their comments hurt.

Second-Hand Stories

I am paraphrasing this true story to remove the dialect so that it will be clear to those who are unfamiliar with our dialect.

Man to me: I know you all owe money to people and you don't want to pay.

Me: *And how do you know that?*

Man: *A friend of mine told me that.*

Me: *And how did your friend know that?*

Man: *His friend told him.*

This was a case of somebody said, that somebody said, that somebody said. And it was fake news.

How often do we get influenced by second-hand stories that we know nothing about? How often do people try to use us to help carry out their grudges against others by feeding us false stories? Their objective is use us to project their prejudices and agendas. Have you ever wondered how many people have negative views of you – judging you – because of what they have been told but without knowing the facts?

Few people have the resources or the inclination to validate what they are being told, so they believe what they hear, especially if it is being told to them by someone they consider to be a friend. That is what happened in the short story I gave above. Not only do they not know, but they also spread stories that they don't know to be true, oblivious of the fact they are being used by somebody else to carry out private mischief. How often do we spread stories or share posts, not knowing whether they are true or not?

Please Don't Judge Me

Second-hand cigarette smoke is bad. It is a killer. And so are second-hand stories. Second-hand stories are dream killers. Sometimes doors are closed to you because of second-hand stories somebody has heard and believed. Second-hand stories wound you in the spirit. They are like ghosts; you don't know where they came from, you don't know who has heard them, and you feel powerless to fight them.

This is why we need to be firmly connected to a supernatural source. Never disconnect from your God and His son Jesus, your Lord and savior. You must always fight for your dream with a partner, the Holy Spirit. Never neglect your prayer life, your fasted life, your giving life, your worship life, and your fellowship life. This is how you fight fake stories and the unfair judgment you get from others. The Lord fights your battles.

Second-hand stories often come laced with self-righteousness; people who perceive themselves morally and spiritually superior to others and give themselves the freedom to apply standards to everyone else. They often speak without empathy and without a proper understanding of another person's circumstances. They come to arbitrary conclusions which they are eager to share with whoever wants to listen or read. The ease and speed of electronic communication and social media posts are fertile soil for second-hand stories and self-righteousness.

Knowing how to compartmentalize the comments that come from self-righteous people is important to dreamers. Otherwise, one can get distracted by trying to respond to unhelpful talk, engaging in constant fire-fighting which diverts valuable time and energy from one's dream.

Dreaming After Divorce

If your marriage has fallen apart, and you are trying to rebuild your life, it's tough to focus on the distractions that come from uninformed comments. It is already a nightmare dealing with a divorce, where will you find the emotional energy to focus on judgmental comments? It is not my intention to discuss the theological and doctrinal teachings on divorce here. I am not referring to the celebrity-type lifestyle where divorce seems to be a pastime.

I am discussing reality: divorce happens. I don't think that most people enter marriage intending to get a divorce. Most people sincerely believe in "till death do us part" or "this is forever." But unfortunately, things sometimes fall apart despite the best intentions at the start. And few things wreck personal dreams as divorce does. Not only does it leave many people emotionally drained, it often leaves people financially damaged and having to start over. Stigmatizing these people, being judgmental, and making them feel like inferior beings are not helpful.

I do not encourage divorce. I think people should make every possible effort to avoid it. I have had the privilege of helping prevent some divorces from happening. I also have not been able to prevent some of them. For those who chose to, or were forced to get divorced, I showed them the same love and respect as anybody else. It is not my role to add more burden to those already laboring under the strain of shattered dreams.

So know that you can still achieve your dreams after divorce; you can bounce back and live an emotionally healthy life. You are not excluded from the happy world; you are not excluded from the church. Do not lose your self-esteem. Do not think that you are worse than anyone else.

If, on reflection, you acknowledge that you may have been primarily responsible for the divorce, for whatever reason, make it right with God. If there is an option to reconcile, do it. If you think you are not responsible, forgive the other party. But after all is said and done, take a realistic look at your life, reassess your situation, and go after your dreams.

I am one of the leaders at Restoration Centre. We believe in presenting the hope of restoration for every life regardless of the situation. We follow the standards set by Jesus. We know He restored a woman who had had five husbands and was with man number six. He administered grace and gave a second chance to a woman who was caught red-handed in adultery. Even though

What Shall We Become of Your Dreams

Zacchaeus was a known corrupt official, He invited Himself into Zacchaeus' house and restored him. Jesus went in search of Peter after Peter made a spectacle of himself, cursing, lying, and denying knowing Him.

Jesus reached out to the most messed-up lives and gave them another opportunity, a second chance to dream. And so should we.

Misjudging Pain

We already established that not everyone will understand your dream; not everyone will be able to see what you see or understand the direction you are going. Because a dream is something you see in your heart, you might even find it difficult to communicate it in words to another person. Since other people often cannot fully understand your dream, they will also be unable to understand the powerful motivation that's driving you. Neither are they likely to understand the intense emotions that arise if you feel that your dream is slipping away.

The Book of First Samuel[46] tells us about Hannah. Hannah's dream was to have a baby but she was having difficulty conceiving. In Hannah's time, the inability to have a child was a major embarrassment to a woman and it was the cause of severe emotional distress. Hannah's embarrassment was aggravated by another woman, Peninnah, who had more than one child. She was

---

46 1 Samuel Chapter 1

making Hannah's life miserable. Peninnah may be described as one of those insensitive and self-righteous persons who found joy in another person's pain.

Every day Hannah was mocked and taunted. The taunts drove her to tears. So distraught was she that she could not eat. Her husband tried to console her, "Why are you crying, Hannah? Why aren't you eating? Why are you so brokenhearted because you have no children? You have me, isn't that better than ten sons?" But Hannah was still not comforted.

As she often did, one day Hannah went to the Tabernacle to pray. She was in deep anguish, crying bitterly as she prayed to the Lord. Eli was the priest and seeing her praying quietly but not hearing what she was saying, he misunderstood and thought she was drunk. He gave her a sharp rebuke, "Must you come here drunk? Throw away your wine!"

And here is a lesson. Not everyone recognizes your pain. Very often we hear the words "I know how you feel" from people giving us support. Those are words of courtesy, and we must appreciate the expression of support. But they really don't know how you feel. They just can't.

Sometimes the person who you most expected to understand you, does not. In Hannah's case, it was the priest. It may be relatives. It may best friends. It may be the boss on the job. It may be, and often is, people in the church. And you experience pain upon pain.

But don't stop dreaming.

Hannah explained to Eli that she was not drunk, she was just very sorrowful and pouring her heart out to the Lord. "Don't think I am a wicked woman," she said. Then Eli made a divine declaration over her life, "Go in peace. God has granted your request." After she heard that, she stopped crying, went home, and started to eat again. And in about nine months afterward, she had a son. Her dream was fulfilled.

There are other important lessons in the story of Hannah and Eli the priest. The priest was mistaken when he accused her of being drunk. The pastor is fallible, and he could make a mistake. Many of the problems that arise between the pastor and the membership, and often between the pastor and the society, stem from the high expectations that we have of pastors. We sometimes forget that they are humans. Whereas congregants expect support, understanding, and forgiveness from the church, we are not so willing to extend the same to pastors.

While the office of the pastor does come with high expectations, we must never lose sight of the reality that they are fallible humans and subject to error sometimes. I don't refer to myself by any titles, and I prefer no title, but others often use titles to address me. Sometimes they refer to me as the "Man of God." Whenever that happens, I remind them that I do not like such noble descriptions, but if it used, the emphasis should be on "Man" and not "God."

Hannah did not get offended when she was unfairly rebuked. Even though she was hurting, she was an emotionally and spiritually stable woman when dealing the priest. Remember in the previous chapter we discussed how emotional instability can ruin your dream. If Hannah had become offended and angry with Eli, she may have done like some modern day people, stormed out of the Tabernacle, and refused to go back. She could have allowed herself to be insulted by the mistake of the priest and lose respect for him. She could have gone back to the community and told them how insensitive that priest was. But she remained calm and explained herself. And her dream was fulfilled. There is victory in being classy.

The same person who mistakenly reprimanded her was the same person who gave her the blessing that led to her dream coming true.

Many other blessings followed from Hannah's association with Eli in spite of the unpleasant misunderstanding at the beginning. Later, Hannah's miracle son Samuel would go to serve the same Eli in the same Tabernacle where Hannah was rebuked. As she continued to go to the Tabernacle, her blessings would be supersized when Eli made additional declarations from God upon her life. She was so blessed that she eventually had a total of six children; she had four boys and two girls – the same woman who was once humiliated because she could not have children.

Imperfect servants of God still hear God's voice. Don't judge them too harshly.

Cry Me a River

Many of the norms, standards and practices that influence modern society, its traditions and customs have come from ages past. Many have been handed down from ancient scriptures and the wisdom of our spiritual predecessors from different religions.

We just discussed how often and how bitterly Hannah cried when she was being mocked. In many cultures, it is not unusual to see, hear, or expect a woman to cry when she is in an emotionally difficult situation.

But men, on the other hand, have been socialized to think that crying is a bad thing; that it is a sign of weakness. Wherever did that come from? It is certainly not supported by the scriptures of the Christian church.

Esau wept. Jacob wept. Joseph wept. David wept. Saul wept. Jesus wept. And on and on... Some of these men were prophets, kings, mighty warriors, and major leaders but they were not

Please Don't Judge Me

ashamed of their tears. So why do men tend to think that crying is a sign of weakness? We have been misled.

And the misleading notion that men are not supposed to cry has made a lot of us men into great pretenders. We suppress our emotions, we cry in secret and pretend that all is well when we step out. We act strong and in control when we are sometimes torn-up on the inside. Repressing strong emotional feelings is not a healthy thing.

However, all of us – men and women – know that in chasing our dreams, we get hit with some really brutal blows. Our head spins, our stomach churns, our spirits are broken and we struggle to hold on. Shedding a tear is not a sign of weakness, it is a sign of humanity. I like to refer to it as an emotional escape route.

There is medical and psychological support for the position that crying is not correlated with weakness. On the contrary, there are studies that show that crying has positive health benefits since it helps reduce stress. And stress has all sorts of negative effects on the human body.

In the business environment, one expects that professionals will be able maintain control over their emotions when dealing with tough business issues. And although there are issues that impinge on the personal in the business environment, many business issues are not personal, so one is not expected to be overt-

What Shall We Become of Your Dreams

ly emotional when contemplating business matters. Therefore, while one won't want to be crying in a business meeting or in the normal course of business at work, in general it is not taboo and should not be considered an embarrassment, especially by "real men."

You will be judged. Unfairly judged.

People who don't know you will have views about you.

But you have a partner. A supernatural partner.

The Holy Spirit.

Therefore, you are covered.

So keep calm and carry on dreaming.

Chapter 14

AGAINST ALL ODDS

"God is not constrained by puny minds that often find solace in superficial symbols of importance that feed their egos and self-importance. We need to see our potential through God's eyes, not through the barriers installed by human society."

Most people like watching movies. That's why the movie industry is a billion-dollar industry. There are lots of things we like about movies apart from the plot itself. The superheroes. The lovely houses. The cars. The setting. The attractiveness of the actors. The lifestyles depicted. The fashion. A lot of different things to different people. However, despite how much we enjoy a movie, or however transfixed we are by what and who we see in it, we can never enter the movie and enjoy any of what we see. We are merely spectators.

Have you ever felt that your actual life can compare to watching a movie? You look around and see all manner of people achieving all sorts of interesting things, but you cannot achieve any of it for yourself. You would like to have the type of success and experiences like other people but somehow the opportunities, the favor, the contacts, the support, the finances are just not there. So you look and admire, but you never seem to be able to create a comparable reality for yourself. You feel like a spectator, watching other peoples' successes while silently wondering, "if only..."

"What does she have that I don't?"

"I wonder how he did it and I could not."

It is not that you don't have a dream. You have lots of dreams, but the odds of achieving them are not in your favor. You some-

What Shall We Become of Your Dreams

times feel like if you were born in a different place, in a different set of circumstances, or to a different family, you may have had a chance at your dream. Sometimes you are even conflicted inside; you don't know if to be jealous, proud, or sad about how others are succeeding while you seem incapable of doing the same. But your unemotional self knows that we ought not to be envious of another person's success, we must rejoice with them; we use others' successes as inspiration, not an opportunity to be jealous.

Truth is, you are right at the stage where the stuff of great dreams is made. The farther you are from your desired future state, the more it qualifies as a dream. The reality is that many people have some natural advantages when pursuing certain dreams. There are a lot of sociological, familial, and financial factors that may appear to make some peoples' lives easier. But the majority of people who achieve their dreams are people who faced tremendous odds, but through their persistence and their faith, they were able to break through and make it.

There are real dreams-come-true stories of people who beat incredible odds. Never underestimate the power of the name of Jesus to open doors and change the direction of one's life. Nothing more fundamentally affects the direction of a human life than for it to be blessed by God and to have His favor upon that life.

Against All Odds

From Rags to Riches

Reflect on the true story of Nella. Nella came from a very poor family in the rural part of her country. She barely got a basic education. She was able to read and write but she was an adult with no recognized certification. Apart from poverty, Nella had to deal with a fractured family and illness.

While still a teenager, she experienced an episode of mental illness and had to be hospitalized for several days. She left home at the age of sixteen and moved-in with one side of her broken family. Nella had big dreams to change her circumstances. But where does someone in these difficult circumstances start to pursue big dreams?

As a result of poverty, family issues, and recurring illness, nothing was in her favor. It was fair to describe it as impossible for her achieve big things. But she did not stop dreaming. She took up a job as a live-in housekeeper with an affluent family in an exclusive neighborhood. After all, with her background, what else was there? She kept that job for a few years and then moved on to become a janitor with a janitorial company. Hardly an improvement, one might say. She was still a bystander in life; still just watching the movie of life with no involvement in it.

But this poor girl still had dreams, big dreams. As a janitor, she saved money from the little she earned and did some additional studies as well. Then one day she got an idea to start her own business. She was at Stage 1 of a dream: birth. The idea was one thing, but she had little savings, no financial backing from anyone and no experience in managing a business. But she was a dreamer. Armed with only her dreams, she went bank-hopping (I invented a term) in an effort to convince someone that her business idea was viable and worthy of financing. She went from bank to bank and was turned down over and over.

But there was something else about Nella. She was strong in faith. She believed in God and at each stage of her life, as difficult as it was, she was trusting God and taking care of the fundamentals: prayer, worship, bible-reading, fellowship, and giving.

After being turned down numerous times by banks, the Lord opened a door. She finally met a banker who was willing to "take a chance on her." "Take a chance" is the everyday expression but to her, it was her prayers being answered. She got some initial capital via a small bank loan and invested it in starting her business – pursuing her dream. She entered the world of entrepreneurship. In business terms, she was taking a major risk in a competitive environment, with no business experience and never having run a business before!

Remember there are some fundamental things about dreaming: partner with the Holy Spirit, believe in yourself, be prepared for tough times, and remember to trust God to help you bounce back when you get knocked down, because you will get knocked down sometimes.

Against All Odds

And so, the poor housekeeper-come-janitor started out as a businesswoman with no prior experience in running a business and no business partner except the Holy Spirit. And her business started to develop. She got more and more clients until, after a few years, she had some of the biggest corporate clients in the country. Soon she had a fairly large staff and a fleet of vehicles. The bankers were now seeking her out to lend her money or to get her to invest. How the tables turned.

She eventually bought a large office complex building in an active business hub. She also acquired her private residential home in one of the country's most exclusive neighborhoods. In terms of assets, she was a multi-millionaire. And yeah, along the way, she earned a Master's Degree from one of the world's most reputable universities. She fought against all odds. And won.

So what shall become of *your* dreams?

Pride and Prejudice

In most countries of the world, perhaps all countries of the world, there are social classes. Among those classes, there are the elites of society; the affluent and the well-connected. There is the upper class, middle class, and the poor, like Nella was. History, often with a helping of prejudice, has created a social structure that in many ways made some people more equal than others, even in the most so-called developed and enlightened societies.

What Shall We Become of Your Dreams

The elites are often defined by race, financial status, career, and yes, religion too. They have created unwritten rules that are exclusionary; "certain people" do not belong in "certain places." It is always an uphill task for the poor to beat the odds. And that is why we need a supernatural partner. I recommend Jesus and the Holy Spirit because I have proven them.

Even Jesus had to deal with societal perceptions and prejudices. After Philip met Jesus, he was excited to share the news with his friend Nathaniel. As recorded by John, "Philip went to look for Nathanael and told him, 'We have found the very person Moses and the prophets wrote about! His name is Jesus, the son of Joseph from Nazareth.'

'Nazareth!' exclaimed Nathanael. 'Can anything good come from Nazareth?'"[47]

Nazareth was not a city recognized by the religious elite as the city of great prophets. Nathanael could not imagine that the person who God chose to fulfill the most important assignment in the history of the world could come from a city like Nazareth. Nathanael had a limited understanding of how God operated.

God is unpredictable. He is not constrained by puny minds that often find solace in superficial symbols of importance that feed their egos and self-importance. We need to see our potential through God's eyes, not through the barriers installed by human

---

47 John 1:45,46 NLT

society. When we do, we understand that the realization of our dreams can circumvent the prejudices of men. This could be one of the reasons that Jesus chose "unlearned and ignorant" people to forever change the course of human history. They would not have stood a chance if they were assessed based on the typical societal or religious hierarchy. God specializes in using the simple things of the world to confound the wise.

In acknowledging one's place in society, one does not have to engage in class warfare. We do not have to be hostile to, or envious of, other people's place in the world. We just need to know that our dreams are achievable regardless of where we find ourselves in the social structure. We can start from behind and still end up winning. We may fall behind sometimes but we bounce back and surge ahead again.

There are many stories throughout history where people faced incredible, sometimes "impossible" odds, but with faith and focus, they persevered and succeeded.

Whereas it is true that some people may appear to have certain advantages, there are some things that are common to all of us, regardless of where we are in the social construct. In a democracy, while the billionaire can use his money to influence voters, ultimately he has only one vote, just like the pauper. While the media might use their platform to spin issues one way or the other, ultimately the producer and the anchor have only one vote each.

The other neutral thing is time. Everybody has twenty-four hours in a day. The person who started at the bottom and climbed all the way to the top had twenty-four hours in each day in order to accomplish that. The person who achieved academic success had twenty-four hours in each day to prepare. If you look carefully enough, you can find people who started at a place comparable to where you are, and they made it. They had the same twenty-four hours that you have. How we use our time makes the difference.

We know that the details of everybody's circumstances are different. But time is still neutral. That's why Ephesians 5:16 (NLT) encourages us to "make the most of every opportunity..." Otherwise translated as "redeeming the time" (KJV). This advice from the Book of Ephesians is what we refer to when we say, "don't waste time" or "don't lose a good opportunity when you get one." Time is one of the most valuable assets that we have! Invest your twenty-four hours wisely.

Thank You, Papa

In an earlier chapter, I spoke of the very humble beginnings our family had. In blunt language, we were poor. Very poor. We had no rich or influential friends and family. We had no influential contacts in society. We had to make it on our own. Right up to my teenage years, these are the things that I did not have: refrig-

Against All Odds

erator, stove, bed, mattress, telephone, electricity, running water, television, radio, internet, car, microwave, cell phone, computer, sometimes no shoes, often without three meals a day, no daily vitamins, and limited clothes. Even toothbrushes and toothpaste were sometimes scarce. My parents did not have permanent jobs. What were the odds of succeeding?

But what I did have was a committed father, a dream, and late in my teenage years, my faith in Jesus. At that early age, I came to the conclusion that if my situation was to change, the power of God's blessings was a key ingredient. I had my earthly father and my heavenly teaming up on my behalf. What a combination!

At the early age about eleven years old, I had to write a key examination. This exam was critical to transitioning to higher education; failing it could have a major impact on the rest of one's life. It was a one-time shot at this exam because it was age-restricted. A teacher at my school tried to deny me the opportunity to write the exam. I won't speculate about his motives, but I had my suspicions. But thank God for a wise and courageous earthly father. He intervened and made representations on my behalf to government, and the teacher's decision was reversed. I passed the exam.

Backed by my father's prayers and a dream in my own little heart, I pushed through the following stages of my life, continuing to study and improve my qualifications.

I saw God open door after door for me. I saw His favor in all sorts of circumstances. I saw Him neutralize haters and those whose minds were not pure. At one point, my employer granted me a scholarship to pursue a master's degree, which I successfully completed. I eventually got to the highest level in my chosen career. As an adult, I have everything that my father did not have. In her pre-teen years, my daughter had everything that I did not have when I was at that stage. It's called generational blessings.

Psalm 112:1-4 (NLT):
"How joyful are those who fear the Lord and delight in obeying his commands.
Their children will be successful everywhere.
An entire generation of godly people will be blessed.
They themselves will be wealthy, and their good deeds will last forever.
Light shines in the darkness for the godly."

Chapter 15

MISTAKEN IDENTITY

"Some believe that you can tell the measure of a man by the way he treats women, whether it is his mother, wife, daughters, or any other woman in his circle."

Mistaken Identity

God has been a "victim" of mistaken identity

by many people. Perhaps it is because of how the church has presented Him. Perhaps it is through misunderstanding. Perhaps it is because of an imprecise distinction between the Old Covenant and the New Covenant. Many of us see God as a strict disciplinarian who is set to swoop down and punish us as soon as we slip, make a mistake, or sin. We have learned to fear God in the literal sense of the word "fear": *an uncomfortable emotion triggered by the threat of danger or harm; to be apprehensive of someone or something that is potentially painful or threatening.*

Is that really who God is? The New Testament reveals God through the person of Jesus Christ and that certainly is not the nature and character of the God who is revealed by Jesus. Jesus was a healer of broken hearts, a friend to the friendless, and an advocate for second chances.

He clearly expressed the standards required by true believers and the need to turn away from a life of sin and unrighteousness, but yet forgiveness and leniency were His trademarks. He was often criticized, not for His harshness, but for His gentleness toward those whom the hardliners of His day considered to be unworthy sinners. He did not condone or encourage wrong, He just chose instead to give second chances and point people to the joy of living right. One can argue that salvation itself – being born again – is a second chance; the "again" in "born again" refers to a second chance. Again is an adverb meaning "another

What Shall We Become of Your Dreams

time; second time; once more."

We often confuse the implications and consequences of our choices, our decisions and our actions with the nature and character of God. Actions and decisions have consequences, and the consequences that are precipitated by our deliberate choices can have results that are either positive or negative. Whether it turns out to be negative or positive, it is not necessarily the work of God; it's just the product of our choices.

The confusion between choices and consequences has also led to mistaking the identity of God.

"How could a loving God put people in hell?" many ask. This is often to discredit the ramifications of the biblical teaching about the implications of turning one's back on God. But a loving God does not *put* people in hell. A loving God has gone to great lengths to explain to people how to have eternal life and *avoid* hell.

When a parent warns a child, "Before crossing the road, look left, then right and then left again before crossing, or you could get knocked down," do we ask how could a loving parent send a child to get knocked down? When parents caution their children that they can die in a crash if they don't wear a seatbelt or if they text and drive or if they disobey the traffic laws, what does it mean? It means a loving parent is providing caring guidance to

Mistaken Identity

the children. And if a child disobeys, the negative consequences are a result of a deliberate choice, not a heartless parent.

So when life gets tough, and dreams appear to be slipping away, don't think that God is making your life miserable by punishing you for something did or didn't do. If you are aware of something that you did or didn't do that may have not been pleasing to God, it quite easy to make it right with Him. A loving parent is always willing to reconcile with his or her children.

If you think that God is not supporting you, it will undermine your self-confidence and will drain your enthusiasm to get up and fight for your dream. Instead of thinking that God is punishing you when things go wrong, think instead of the promise that all things work together for the good of those who love the Lord. He will find a way to manage things, even the bad things, in a way that ultimately works out in your favor.

Based on the biblical record, Jesus was always willing to respond to people's needs. We just have to take a step toward Him. A woman who was hemorrhaging for twelve years *went* to him and got her answer. A blind man sitting at the side of the road *shouted out* to Him and got his sight back. Some men *ripped off* part of a roof to reach Him, and they got their answer. A gentleman by the name of Nicodemus *got up* late at night and *went* in search of Jesus. He too got his answer. They all took a deliberate action to reach Him.

Make your move.

There are many more examples. He is not unwilling to respond to you. Just take a step toward Him. It is not wise to shut God out of your life but still want all that He has to offer. If you take one step toward Him, He takes two steps toward you. Do what you have to do, and you will find a willing heart welcoming you.

The evidence suggests that there is a special place in the heart of God for hurting and heartbroken people, people whose unfortunate circumstances have put them at a disadvantage. Among the things that Jesus said in outlining his mission statement was, "I came to heal the brokenhearted."[48] For example, there was a man who was trying to get healed for thirty-eight years! There was a multitude of sick people who were also trying to get healed in the same place where this man was. But the record shows that Jesus approached that man and healed only him. What made the difference? I think it was his loneliness; he was in a disadvantageous position. He was there suffering for thirty-eight years because he had no one to help him. The people who had the help of others were getting healed ahead of him. He kept trying all by himself without success for all those years.

When you find yourself in a position where you have no help and you are struggling to make it in a hostile world all by yourself, remember that God has His eyes on you. He empathizes with your situation, and more importantly, He can come to your

---

48 Luke 4:18 KJV

rescue. In that sense, you are never dreaming alone.

There are numerous other stories of Jesus singling out hurting people from a crowd, disrupting His schedule or going out of His way to reach them. He went about using some very familiar phrases, "Fear not" and "Be of good cheer" were two of His favorite phrases. He was a comforter. He was not a strict task-master who went around condemning people. The people He chastised were the hypocrites, not the hurting. Some people are weak, and some people are wicked. He knows the difference.

Chivalry is Not Dead

Another example of Jesus's concern for the hurting is His attention to hurting women. The need to cherish and protect our women has long been a part of our civility and good manners. Some believe that you can tell the measure of a man by the way he treats women, whether it is his mother, wife, daughters, or any other woman in his circle. To many people, that quality of gentlemanliness and finesse is referred to as chivalry, which is defined as an honorable and polite way of behaving, especially toward women.

Jesus was especially kind to women. At one time a group of men made a citizens' arrest and took a woman to Jesus for some sort of judgment because they caught her in the act of adultery.[49]

---

49 John Chapter 8

What Shall We Become of Your Dreams

They publicly humiliated her. They were ready to stone her to death for her crime. Observe that they brought the woman but not the man. Certainly, if she was caught red-handed, there must have been a man involved. But the man was conveniently let off the hook.

But Jesus was having none of it. He took no part in this plot to destroy the woman. Instead, He exposed the hypocrisy of her accusers, the men, by turning their attention to their own sins. If Jesus was a chauvinistic male, He may have been delighted to talk-down to the woman because of her lifestyle. He would have gone on a "mansplaining" rant. But He let her go. He gave her a second chance to live a different life. What nobility.

This approach was repeated in a similar fashion many times. There was a time when He met a woman who had had five previous husbands and was involved with a sixth man.[50] He had a fairly long discourse with her about social and religious issues, and even though He specifically mentioned her multiple relationships, He did not do so in a manner that was condescending or humiliating.

Once again, He looked to the future; His concern was the future and not the past. If I could paraphrase His approach to these women, it would be Him saying, "You have not lived your best life, you are not living your best life right now. You have a second chance, go change your life and chart a new course."

50 John Chapter 4

Mistaken Identity

There are many times when a woman's choices, mistakes, or faulty judgments result in outcomes that are not ideal. To another person, she may be the subject of ridicule, gossip, and criticism. It is often difficult for people who have lived a sheltered or "normal" life to understand the different path another life has taken. And it is not always because someone is consciously carefree, irresponsible or promiscuous. There are other reasons such as upbringing, self-image, mental issues, or spiritual issues that may result in what appears to be a woman's "bad choices" or a woman who repeatedly trusts the wrong men. And there are times when it is none of those things; things just don't work out, in spite of some women's best efforts.

When faced with scenarios where her private life is the subject of open derision, it could be very challenging for a woman to muster the strength to bounce back and pursue her dreams. However, apart from her personal strength of character, she must understand that there is a God of love and forgiveness who believes in second chances. When she embraces the opportunity to create a new future with the Holy Spirit as her partner, the possibilities are endless. The personal challenges or shortcomings of the past will fade into irrelevance when His blessings start to flow.

Jesus' sensitivity to a woman's pain is unmistakable. On the way to be crucified, while He was being beaten, while He was bloodied and being mocked, He still paused to comfort the crying women at the side of the road. At another time He stopped a

What Shall We Become of Your Dreams

large, bustling crowd as if to say, "Hold on. Stop. I am hearing a woman crying." He stopped a funeral procession, raised the woman's son from the dead, and gave him back to his mother. He stopped her crying. He has an ear for the hurting.

Not all lives follow the idealistic, fairy tale path.
Some go through a very chaotic and non-traditional road.
But God is a sensitive God.
He focuses on the potential of your future.
Your future shall be better than your past.
Go for it!

CPSIA information can be obtained
at www.ICGtesting.com
Printed in the USA
LVHW052037280122
709444LV00013B/990